THE LEADER COACH: EXPOSING YOUR SOUL

by
Don Levin and Terry Edwards

Bloomington, IN  Milton Keynes, UK

AuthorHouse™
1663 Liberty Drive, Suite 200
Bloomington, IN 47403
www.authorhouse.com
Phone: 1-800-839-8640

AuthorHouse™ UK Ltd.
500 Avebury Boulevard
Central Milton Keynes, MK9 2BE
www.authorhouse.co.uk
Phone: 08001974150

© 2007 Don Levin and Terry Edwards. All rights reserved.

No part of this book may be reproduced, stored in a retrieval system, or transmitted by any means without the written permission of the author.

First published by AuthorHouse 2/22/2007

ISBN: 978-1-4259-8886-9 (sc)

Printed in the United States of America
Bloomington, Indiana

This book is printed on acid-free paper.

Contents

Preface   1

How do two guys who don't know each other but share a passion for leadership and coaching come together to write a book, much less this one. Why write it at all?

PART I: Essentials: The Leader and Soul Defined   7

Defining the Leader Coach and examining the manner in which the Leader Coach must look within himself to discover his inner being. Introduction of the Leader Coach Evolution Model.

Chapter 1: Defined   11

Defining the Leader Coach, and contrasting him from the Manager and the Leader. The Leader Coach is on the field with the players, as opposed to coaching from the sidelines. The paid for hire Executive Coach is beyond the scope of this work. This is largely a one-on-one proposition in which boundaries have to be set and expectations have to be agreed upon between the Leader Coach and the Player.

Chapter 2: Internal   23

The Leader Coach within – what it takes! Answering the question: Are you ready to be Leader Coach? What contrasts coaching from mentoring, and the sacred nature of the coaching relationship? The impact of the glass ceiling within the corporate structure that incents the promotion of technical people to that of leader, and gives rise to the Peter Principle of rising to one's level of incompetence.

PART II: Foundation: Lessons in Leadership   37

With the focus on the Leader Coach, what are the attributes that are absolutely critical for success in this endeavor? Three models of leadership that we have encountered in our careers that appear to define the skills requisite to the role.

Chapter 3: Congruence   40

The first model presented for consideration is that espoused by Kouzes & Posner, and it is known as the Leadership Congruence Model. It contains the elements of Encourage the Heart, Modeling the Way, Inspiring a Shared Vision, Challenging the Process, and Enabling Others to Act. Like the Olympic Rings, we attempt to refine the behavior of the leader so that the rings align and are in congruence.

Chapter 4: Courage   51

A significant attribute that makes a leader into a Leader Coach is that of courage. The Leader Coach has to have the requisite courage to deliver difficult feedback, to make difficult decisions, and to admit to when they are challenged. The Leader Coach must have the courage to dare, to care enough to face risks, and to deal with fear and the manner in which it impacts decision making.

Chapter 5: Modeling   65

We believe the single largest component of the Leader Coach is his character, or in other words, his soul. Does he possess the attributes needed to command the respect of his subordinates and turn them into followers? Contained within the U.S. Army's Model of Leadership, are the attributes of Be, Know, and Do.

PART III: Preparation: Personal Attributes of a Leader Coach   73

Because the Leader Coach is intimately involved with the Player, it is imperative that a very firmly defined relationship is established, nourished, and continues to grow throughout the journey. These chapters present an opportunity to become more introspective and to conduct additional self-analysis.

Chapter 6: Heart   77

The Leader Coach has to be a Servant Leader and has to love his people – agape – love as a verb, and while doing so, be willing to expose his soul and to risk being hurt. Success comes through when he desires only the best for his team member, and derives satisfaction from the act of coaching (self-actualization).

Chapter 7: Presence   85

The Leader Coach has to be there; not just physically, but emotionally and mentally too. It is imperative that the Leader Coach has the courage to admit when he is not totally present, and to make alternative arrangements so as to eliminate distractions in environment, time management, and personal issues.

Chapter 8: Risk   93

Supportive Intervention is all about caring enough about the Player so as to risk the relationship. At times, the Leader Coach will be forced to use tough love.

PART IV: Practice: The Art of Conversation   103

The actual coaching relationship is all about the series of conversations that take place between the Leader Coach and the Player. All are important and feed off of one another.

Chapter 9: Involved   107

The first of the three conversations that a Leader Coach has to be able to have with his team member is the "Social" conversation. The Leader Coach must demonstrate genuine interest in the lives of those whom he leads. This begins with a personal knowledge of family, outside interests, hobbies, and ancillary challenges with immediate and extended family.

Chapter 10: Resolved — 123

The second of the three conversations that a Leader Coach has to be able to have with his team member is known as the "Performance" conversation. The Leader Coach has to resist the urge to 'mentor' by sharing how "he did it", and must rely upon the use of the Socratic Method. Coaching asks more questions than it provides answers.

Chapter 11: Evolved — 145

The third of the three conversations that a Leader Coach has to be able to have with his team member is known as the "Developmental" conversation. This is where Supportive Intervention comes into play; the team member has to take responsibility for his or her performance, and true growth takes place. Both the Leader Coach and the Player have to expose their hearts and souls by showing mutual concern and involvement.

PART V: Enhancements: Exponential Gifts of the Leader Coach — 169

By definition, an enhancement is something that improves or makes greater. The last three gifts that a Leader Coach provides to his players are those of energy, ownership, and giving.

Chapter 12: Energy — 173

It remains incumbent upon the Leader Coach to instill the energy into the group. Not all of it, certainly not all of the time, but a constant source – much like the eternal flame. It is about being the Nucleus, and is achieved by being visible and accessible; by being real, and bringing passion, fun, and making it real for the team. By setting the tone, and by being the constant True North from which everyone takes their lead.

Chapter 13: Ownership — 181

Who really owns the coaching relationship, and who really gets the coaching. We can't want it more than they do! How do we know whom to invest our time into? When is it time to pull the plug on the relationship?

Chapter 14: Giving   **189**

To really give of yourself as a Leader Coach it is imperative that you escape from the Ivory Tower and the White Board and to get out from behind the desk. Passing it [coaching] on and down to the people who really need it, requires a willing heart.

PART VI: Finale: Assessment and Final Thoughts   **197**

To assist you in determining just where you fit into the entire Manager- Leader- Leader Coach spectrum, we have a final theory called The Leadership Coaching Coefficient Triangle.

Chapter 15: Assess   **201**

The roles of Manager, Leader, and Leader Coach are not mutually exclusive. How all three components are balanced is of paramount importance to the success enjoyed by the leader coach, the player, as well as the organization. Where do you fit on the Leadership Coaching Coefficient Triangle. Try a 360 and find out!

Epilogue   **212**

Being a Leader Coach is both the hardest, yet most rewarding work that a leader can engage in. Everyone may think that they can do it, but the proof is in the pudding. Coaching is the greatest gift that we can give to a member of our team, and when done properly, it does expose our own soul, and has the ability to become our legacy.

Bibliography   **215**

"I cannot live without books." Thomas Jefferson to John Adams.

About the Authors   **219**

PREFACE

So how is that two guys who didn't know each other end up writing a book together? The short answer is networking. The longer answer is Fred Esposito, and the coaching and encouragement that he brings to a bunch of entrepreneurs at bi-weekly meetings. A great cheerleader in his own right, Fred brings out the best in the group. After a conversation about what Fred calls "handles" or things to take away as action items, Terry's was, "I want to write a book some day." This was quickly met with a direction from Fred for Terry to talk to Don, who has the distinction of having published a couple of novels. How's that for a shameless plug. Well, not too shameless since we didn't even mention the titles! But we digress. Don's brilliant and insightful question to Terry was, "when is some day," and a luncheon appointment was established for two days later. One lunch was followed by two more, and the rest we say is history. Thanks Fred for being present, and for being a coach worthy of emulation.

Because inquiring minds always want to know, the title of the book was born in the course of the very first meeting because it really captured the essence of the passion that was sitting there amidst the sushi, wasabi, and pita wraps. A subsequent review of the outline by a trusted colleague brought to light the question of why we would dare to use "exposing your soul" as part of the title; it is so bold a statement, and we may have served our purposes by simply utilizing something milder such as "heart on your sleeve" or some other less passionate or risky visual. The answer: while it is an intimidating title, so is the very topic about which we are writing. There are many leaders. They come in all shapes and sizes. Some are managers. Some are organizers. Some are doers. Some are dreamers. Some are administrators. Some are delegators or facilitators. Some are mentors. Some are even *great* mentors. Some are great leaders simply because of the manner in which they influence their people. Most assuredly, not all of them are coaches. Some fancy themselves to be coaches. Some aspire to be coaches. But, the proof, as they say, is in the pudding.

This is probably a good time to clarify that this book is written for the leader coach and his follower(s), and not the professional executive coach. Why write it you ask? Several reasons actually.

First, it is our own heartfelt belief that the Leader Coach is truly the unsung hero in the trenches. As we sat at our customary table at Starbucks, often times entertaining the folks sitting at nearby tables with our passionate arm waving and table pounding, and writing on the glass window with Vis-a-Vis marker, and discussed the real payoff to coaching, we realized that true coaching is really a selfless act of kindness, and that the coach comes away a better person for his efforts as well.

Second, that it is very fashionable in today's corporate environment for top executives to be afforded the luxury of a personal coach, and that some executives engage the services of these coaches, or have them assigned to them, as either a reward or as a status symbol. We believe that these are the wrong reasons. While these coaches most assuredly provide a valuable service to these *very* fortunate individuals, *unfortunately*, the fruit of this coaching often stays only at the highest levels within the organization. This is neither the coach's, nor the player's (executive's) fault, but is largely attributable to the shortcomings of the organization. So, while it is a gift to the individual receiving the coaching, it often begins and ends there. Therefore, while we both acknowledge and salute these coaches and their efforts, that form of coaching is completely different, and, with a little bit of luck, may be addressed in a subsequent work. Our goal in this modest offering, is to recognize and assist the leader who is also a coach, and is found at virtually every level of every organization. We hope that in some small measure that this work will be of assistance to this lionhearted Leader Coach.

That being said, we fervently believe that the role of Leader Coach is not for the faint of heart. It is most assuredly the most difficult task of a leader. Again relating back to the same Starbucks discussion, we believe that to be an effective Leader Coach, you do have to expose your own soul to the process, and risk both your relationship, and your standing, with the player. This element of risk is an inevitable and completely unavoidable part of the process. We can assure you however that the risk is worth the investment based on what we receive in return. This give and take, the accompanying highs and lows, as well as potential risk is like the old adage, "to have a friend, be a friend," or "to get a letter, write a letter," so too is it with coaching, and there in lies the beauty of it all.

Certainly, the best way to learn something is to teach it. When the student is ready, the teacher appears. So it is with the coaching relationship. When a leader takes the step in becoming a Leader Coach, it is inevitable that he too will grow and benefit from the process.

As leaders within several Fortune 200 companies, we both have had the pleasure of being mentors and coaches, as well as to have been mentored and coached ourselves. The beauty of being both a teacher and a student is that the Journey never ends. While the destination is important, it really is all about the Journey. It is funny how it takes years and years to learn this basic truth. Apparently that is why we have perfect 20-20 hindsight. As Yogi Berra is reported to have said, "when you come to a fork in the road, take it." With that added piece of wit and brilliance, it must be time for a disclaimer of sorts. While we hope that each reader will take away action items that they are both comfortable and confident with implementing, there are no magic instructions or silver bullets associated with Leader Coaching. Each relationship will be like a snowflake; no two will be alike. It is based on true servant leadership, and the love that a leader feels for the people that he serves within the organization.

We would also like to acknowledge that there has been a host of wonderful books written on leadership, management, coaching, intervention, motivation, teamwork, development, interpersonal relationships, and communications, as well as a plethora of related topics. We should know, because if it is in print, between us, we've probably read it. If you can't find the book at Barnes & Noble, try one of our bookshelves ... we probably have it! We even compiled a bibliography of a few of the ones that have influenced us in the preparation of this book. Why spend airplane rides, vacation, and other idle time reading about these topics? Because, leadership and coaching are two things that we are very passionate about, hence the public displays at Starbucks and other eateries that have prompted a steady rotation of meeting sites. With that said, and as a stated premise, it is our desire to make our own modest contribution to the art of leadership and coaching. Not solely intended as a rehash of what is currently out there, but perhaps a new perspective that provides the reader with one gold nugget with which to forge a new relation, improve an existing one, or to simply make their piece of the vineyard that much more fertile. We remain confident that *The Leader Coach: Exposing Your Soul* will present the reader with food for thought and a new way of approaching this vital issue.

A final disclaimer, and one that we do not take lightly. As we said a few pages back, managers and leaders, as well as coaches, come in a variety of shapes, sizes, colors, and *genders*. As we began writing the body of this work, we were both concerned with how to address the 'gender issue.' By this, we mean what is the proper manner in which to address the whole politically correct use of pronouns. A random survey of people that we know indicated that 'he' is the gender neutral, socially acceptable form for the manuscript. Some of the women that we asked even went so far as to tell us very pointedly that *they* found it both offensive, patronizing, and even a form of pandering, when authors go out of their way to use the feminine pronouns. Further, that this obsession with being PC is actually a distraction from the actual content of the book, which should remain of predominant importance. Others pointed out that the idea of alternating the use of he and she between chapters was darn right stupid. So much for asking the studio audience what they think! This left us in a real quandary.

A search on the internet led us to several sites. McGraw Hill advised we should use 'they', 'them', or 'their' and only use 'he' or 'she' when referring to a specific male or female. Prentice-Hall advised us to treat men and women impersonally and to avoid sexism at all costs. Technical Writer advised us to bypass the problem of gender whenever possible by utilizing the second person (you) rather than the third person (he, she) or to avoid pronouns completely.

In any event, we have now spent nearly a page of this text attempting to share with you, the reader, the inner workings of our dilemma.

Because we are certain that you are reading this book with more of an eye towards the content of our message, and because neither one of us is in any manner, shape, or form a sexist, we have determined to not worry about this issue, but wanted you to know that we considered it, indeed fretted over it, and resolved that the true professional will recognize the true sincerity of our message, and desire to share the gift of coaching.

Like Dorothy's odyssey to garner an audience with the Wizard of Oz, we are seeking the attributes of Courage, Heart, Thought, Energy, Congruence, and the ability to discern all that is good around us, and to share these qualities with the people that we care about most. The art of conversation is quickly becoming lost to our society as we place increasing reliance on technological advancements in wireless communications that allow us to send e-mails and photographs through our computers, as well as text messaging from our telephones. We hope that this body of work will be of some modest form of assistance to all those leaders who dare to expose their souls and to assume the mantel of leader coach.

Don Levin

Terry Edwards

PART I

*Essentials:
The Leader and Soul Defined*

After finishing the Preface, you may have a good idea of what to expect from this book. We wanted to make certain that it was clear that this book is directed to the Leader who desires to become a Leader Coach, and is *not* about the Executive Coach. The Executive Coach indeed plays a very valuable role in the professional world of business and sports, but is not the scope of this work.

In this part of the book we are going to define the Leader Coach, and examine the manner in which a Leader Coach must look within himself to discover his inner being. We are also going to examine the premise of our Leader Coach Evolution Model, and how the focus of the Leader Coach's attention shifts from himself to filling the needs of his followers.

We also believe that the diagrams located in chapter 2 will illustrate what we believe separates the Manager from the Leader, and the Leader from the Leader Coach. Going beyond merely a focus on self to that of others in terms of attention, it is also about the spectrum of opportunity that presents itself to the Leader Coach when through the application of his time, he can shift his player(s) from a results focused orientation to one of New Possibilities.

While one can certainly *choose* to become a Leader Coach, it is only possible to do so *after* having mastered the skills of the manager and the leader.

CHAPTER 1

Defined

Much has been written and much has yet to be written about Leadership and the Leader. Our endeavor is not to step into the broad topic of Leadership, with its many nuances of strategy, organizational design and structure, execution, and various management practices and styles. Rather, our focus will be on what we believe is the least developed skill of many of today's even most proclaimed leaders, the art of people development, or *coaching*, and more specifically, the role that the leader plays as a coach to his or her team.

There is absolutely no doubt that 'Leader Coach' is a loaded term, and quite frankly, probably means something different to all who hearken to the call. Each of us has vivid images of great leaders and great coaches that have either directly or indirectly influenced our lives, or the times in which we have lived. These leaders and coaches come from all walks of life, professions, and humanistic roles. When you hear the word *leader*, who is it that comes into your mind to personify this powerful word? Take a minute, and think about it. Who is the *leader* that most comes to mind for you? As we have conducted experiments in a variety of settings, we have found that the response to this seemingly straightforward question has ranged from heads of state to local figures of whom you and I have never heard. They could include: Martin Luther King, Jr., Mother Theresa, George Washington, Jesus Christ, or Mahatma Gandhi, Cal Ripken Jr, Nelson Mandella, and on and on. Amazingly, this is just the *personification* of the word. Try typing the question, "what is a leader?" into Google, or any other search engine, and you'll receive about 211,000,000 responses. Bottom line: there is no right or wrong answer to this question. It is as individual as the number of people to whom you ask the question.

A similar inquiry about coaches, and our minds and memories lead us to think of giants such as Knute Rockne, Vince Lombardi, Tom Landry, and a host of others.

For purposes of this exercise, the most simplistic answer, and the premise from which we are operating, is that a Leader is a person who *compels* another person to *want* to follow. Two simple words separate the wheat from the chaff; *compels* and *want*. Many managers and people in positions of power motivate subordinates and get results by resorting to tactics that promote fear, or simply rely upon the raw power associated with the position they hold. In these scenarios, it is the rare person who is able to *compel* another to *want* to follow them. We have all worked with people like this, and recognize that they are not someone that we would willingly subject ourselves, our character, or our careers to except as a last resort. For this reason, the term leadership, especially when utilizing this definition, becomes very personal. It cries out to our values and the very essence of our beliefs, and is another reason that all players have every right to expect that their coaches will be people of high character, great strength, and personify the tenets of courageous leadership.

Pick any modern day politician and view the differences of opinion that the mere mention of his or her name will evoke from people in the office, around the holiday dinner table, or across the country. Blue state, red state, conservative, liberal, ethical, non-ethical, its all a matter of perspective, paradigms, and beliefs. The politician's closest followers, believe with their whole heart and being, that the person they are supporting and working for *is* the answer to our political problems. Yet, at the same moment there are those that live in a state of diametric opposition to this person and his/her political beliefs. Fortunately, in our democratic two-party system, where majority rules, even those regarded as the greatest leaders never were followed in unanimity, nor were they handicapped from leading because of it. Nonetheless, there was a special something that these leaders had at their disposal that compelled their followers to want to follow.

Much has been written about, and even debated, as to whether leaders are naturally born, or can be created. The good news, and the other "ah-ha" for us, as we assembled this definition, is that *anyone* can become a leader. Anyone. If, and granted, it's a big if, they have the heart, the desire, and the willingness to work hard, and more importantly, to expose their soul. Be it as a parent, teacher, manager, scoutmaster, friend, neighbor, subordinate, or work peer – any of the folks in these roles can *compel* another to *want* to follow a direction that he espouses because of the relationship. We believe that it is this very difference in the nature of relationships found in the workplace that separates the manager from the leader. We promise you that there is more to come on the manager vs. leader later. Suffice to say that we believe that managers manage *things* and true leaders lead *people*.

We've discussed the term leader, now how do we tack on the word coach? Even among the world's greatest leaders, few actually fill the role of Leader Coach. Again, leaders compel others to want to follow them. Yet, that does not mean that followers are completing their assignments with the needed quality their role demands, or to the best of their ability, or reaching their full potential, solely because they are allegedly being influenced by a leader. Exercising their will to follow a leader, is merely the first step in the establishment of a coaching relationship. That's where the coach steps up and in.

We asked you before to consider those that you admire as leaders, now we'll ask you to challenge yourself and document some of the best coaching that you have either personally experienced or indirectly witnessed. For sports fans it might be Red Auerbach, Vince Lombardi, Bill Walsh, or a plethora of the great baseball managers that seemingly play musical chairs at the end of each season. For self-helpers it might include Dr. Andrew Weil, Dr. Wayne Dyer, Anthony Robbins, or Zig Ziglar. For each of us, there are probably one to five people from our past that we could label as a critical coach in our lives. Someone that we called upon that we trusted at a critical moment in our lives to help us be the best that we could be, or the best that we could be in addressing a specific issue or opportunity in our lives. It might have been a sports coach, a history teacher, a chaplain, an insightful friend, a parent, a spouse, or even one of our own children. Never under estimate the lessons that we can learn through the innocence of a child of any age.

In business today, Executive Coaching has become a critical function in many corporate-level offices, and we'll briefly touch upon the role of the Executive Coach later. As noted in the preface, this form of coaching is different than the focus of this work. The largest distinction between the two roles is that the Executive Coach is largely on the sidelines and engages in coaching only before or after action. An example of this would be United States Tennis Association (USTA) tennis matches, where there are strictly enforced rules against coaching during a match, even to the point that hand signals and body movements can not be shared between coach and player. As a result of this imposed limitation, the coach has no direct ability to impact the match results, and therefore is also denied direct responsibility for the results of the team or individual he is coaching except in the actual preparation.

The Leader Coach on the other hand is on the field *with* the player. The Leader Coach is also ultimately accountable for the results achieved by those on his team. This is where the magic lies, and what makes this role so impactful, and hopefully attractive, to those of you either already in the role, or contemplating entering the arena. As we have said, it is not for the faint of heart. Success can also be met with disappointment. However, as Theodore Roosevelt wrote years ago:

"[T]here is always a tendency to believe that a hundred small men can furnish leadership equal to to that of one big man. That is not so...Nothing can fully take the place of the indispensable work of leadership."

The role of Leader Coach is incredibly rewarding, yet is chosen and performed by only a few. Just look at how the role of player-coaches has virtually disappeared from nearly all professional sports. At the same time, even in it's hey day, there were only a few that could rise to the challenge. By definition, a player-coach or player-manager was an individual who simultaneously participated as a player while also serving as either a head coach or assistant coach for the team. Still found in semi-pro or amateur ranks, as well as in foreign sports leagues, the role has largely disappeared from American sports.

Yet for many decades, the player-coach was very commonly found in professional basketball. NBA Hall of Famers Bill Russell and Lenny Wilkens, to mention just a couple, were in fact *rostered* player-coaches. In the mid 1970's this was a common practice mainly because of financial restrictions, and was considered as a cost-saving measure by many struggling teams. Today, the collective bargaining agreement between the NBA and the players' union prohibits the use. Nonetheless, Bill Russell the coach, achieved great success because of Bill Russell the player, stunning the world by winning the championship the last year that he played.

Major League baseball can also boast some name players who were also either a coach or a manager while at the end of their respective playing careers. Yogi Berra was a Player-Coach for the New York Yankees in 1963, and Pete Rose was the Player-Manager for the Cincinnati Reds from 1984-1986, achieving success both on the field and in the dugout. Since that time, contracts, and more defined roles for managers, coaches, and players has precluded this from occurring again.

Hopefully the success enjoyed by such notable player coaches will encourage you to want to step into this role. We certainly have enjoyed our respective times in the tank! In fact, our experience is that being the Leader Coach is what makes the role of leader both interesting and meaningful. But, stepping into the role of Leader Coach is not a whimsical decision. This role comes with responsibilities beyond those found in the job descriptions of the Leader or the Manager. For an elaboration on what these added responsibilities entail, please read on, and we hope to both enlighten and inspire you. But for now, some more basics.

Terms

Before we go much further we should settle on a lexicon that we'll be using for the remainder of this book. Terms that we have used and will continue to use include:

- **Leader:** The person that is setting an organization's direction and compelling others to want to follow for any of a litany of reasons.
- **Manager:** The person that has administrative responsibility for a job or function, and directs the work of others to complete necessary components of this logistical or functional responsibility.

- **Mentor:** The person who can provide assistance to a player by sharing experiences and technical skills.
- **Coach:** The person who helps others reach more of their potential.
- **Leader Coach:** Read on and you'll find out, but it includes cool stuff like: motivating, inspiring, and influencing behavior. Being able to leap buildings in a single bound is also not beyond the realm of possibility!
- **Player:** The person the Leader Coach is coaching and leading, and the recipient of this motivation, inspiration, and behavior modification.
- **Subordinate:** The person whose work is directed by a Manager or Leader.

Manager vs. Leader

We discussed earlier how Leaders differ from Managers. It is not our intention to make "Manager" a derogatory term, in fact we see filling the role of Manager (in the work place at least) to be a prerequisite to becoming a Leader. The manager fills the critical role of facilitating and directing the performance of subordinates while ostensibly controlling resources. This role is administrative in nature, and in essence exists to insure that the work actually gets done. Plans are developed, projects are launched, work is delivered, and status is reported. Sounds like a lot of fun right?

From a people development perspective, the manager insures subordinates receive feedback on the quality of their work products, performance appraisals, and either merit or cost of living increases that adhere to established and published company policy. All of these managerial tasks in the realm of people leadership are critical, but remain largely administrative in nature. Insuring that these basics are addressed are the minimum requirement, and the foundation for any superior-subordinate (Leader Coach-Player) relationship to exist and persist. Failing in these fundamental personnel tasks will insure that a manager's tenure and credibility with the player(s) will most assuredly be a short one. Players need to know that they can rely on their managers to meet their basic [organizational] needs. Likewise, not completing these tasks will also brand the manager a failure insofar as the organization is concerned, because it too relies upon the manager to complete these basic tasks. Another limitation that will occur in the absence of these tasks being completed in a timely manner is that the relationship between the manager and player cannot go any deeper, much less become more committed, because the basic needs of the player are not being addressed. That's why we see filling the role of the Manager as a prerequisite to that of becoming a Leader. Without the foundation of being able to do one's basic role, the move to the higher level of relationship – Leader, is not possible. Of course, taking that relationship even an additional step, to that of Leader Coach, would surely remain beyond the realm of possibility.

THE FIELD OF COACHING AND THE LEADER COACH

We discussed the role of Executive Coach earlier and the advantages it offers senior leaders and teams in our work place today. Coaching is truly coming of age, and many of the topics we discuss in this book are based on a few of the general premises within the field of Coaching. The field of Coaching is a study and practice where Terry has had some formal training and experience, yet we don't approach this work from the perspective of the "paid-for-hire" Executive Coach. What we are more interested in is the role of the Leader as Coach. So how do we define "The Coach?" The most basic definition of a Coach that we can come up with is: someone that *partners* with a player to help the player be the *best* at *what the player intends*. In this way, the Executive Coach and the Leader Coach are pursuing the same goal, to wit: "helping the player be the best at what he or she intends." Examining our definition, there are three loaded components namely *partners, best,* and *what the player intends*. Although each of these concepts will be fleshed out with more detail later, we'd like to briefly describe why we feel these are loaded terms.

- **Partner:** United with another in an activity. Approaches an activity and a relationship with a degree of mutuality, where both are working together. This level of mutuality differs significantly from the superior-subordinate relationship where the superior directs the focus of the subordinate.

- **Best:** Of the highest quality. The key to this attribute is that the term Best is defined and measured by the player's abilities and not the leader's assessment. At some later time, if the player's best and the leader's assessment of the player's needed best are not aligned, then the leader may need to make other decisions about the player's viability for the role. This sensitive area is one of the most critical when the Leader becomes the Leader Coach.
- **Player Intent:** We will discuss Intention in detail later, but the aim of coaching is to help the player define what it is that they want to achieve (their intention), and to then help them achieve it to the best of their ability. Again, this is not necessarily where the leader's intention is placed.

The Leader Coach is...

Simply put, the Leader Coach is the Leader who chooses to take the additional step and becomes a Coach. Heretofore we've used the term coaching to mean that aspect of leadership involved with people development. But, the Leader Coach approach goes beyond people development. It is a way of leading, not just in the realm of people development, but also in the areas of performance, planning, and management. In the coaching approach to development, the Coach works with the player to help uncover answers, insights, and approaches that would best serve him in his own development. By this, we mean that coaching conversations are not directive in nature. The Coach's goal is for the player to uncover the direction and put the actions (as identified by the player) in place that will help the player achieve what he or she intends. An example of this is the manner in which law schools rely upon the Socratic Method to help the student garner an appreciation of legal and scholarly principles through a practice of asking the student questions rather than supplying information through direct lecturing.

In the typical leader relationship, the Leader directs the Player to take a certain action, which the Player is compelled to deliver. When the Leader steps into a Leader Coach relationship, the Leader Coach actually challenges the Player with the intent of uncovering the direction or action that is required for the Player to be a successful contributing member of a project, team, or to address specific performance issues. We will discuss the mechanics of this leadership style in Chapter 10, which comes with incredible benefit. By taking coaching beyond what is typically viewed as a developmental conversation and into performance conversations, new "right" answers are uncovered for both the leader and the player. And, the player is able to contribute at a much greater level in the direction of the business and in his or her role.

The Leader Coach is not...

The most difficult aspect of this approach to leadership is establishing purposeful and constructive habits. We have both led large organizations with corresponding level of responsibilities. With these responsibilities came the pressure to deliver. It is unrealistic for the Leader to always play the Leader Coach role. In fact it would be more accurately termed an approach rather than a role. Plain and simple, there will be times when the Leader will need to take command and use a directive style. There will be times when the Leader needs to be a good Manager. There will be times when the Leader Coach may desire to have a coaching conversation, but the player is not willing to be coached. And lastly, there will be times when the player wants to be coached, but the Leader will need to make the call that coaching would be inappropriate for this relationship at this time. So, let's not confuse all of these roles; what allows the leader to comfortably shift from one role, or attitude, to another, is that he is in congruence, has earned the respect of his team, and knows the needs of those whom he serves. These are all additional terms that we will define in great detail in later chapters. Our focus throughout this book will be on that beautiful moment when the Leader is also the Coach. And it is in these moments of leadership when two souls will be exposed.

A Commitment with Boundaries

We'd love to close the chapter and move on after building to such a powerful and touching moment, but there are some additional things we need to discuss about the Leader Coach-Player relationship before we move on.

The first concern is that the Leader Coach role may not be appropriate for every person you lead. This is largely a one-on-one proposition. The first thing we learn as Coaches in that there has to be a coaching contract established between the Coach and Coachee (player). There is no coaching relationship unless the player wants to be coached. Therefore, this is very personal, and not a role to be taken on, or entered into, lightly.

The second concern we have is the establishment of boundaries. When it comes to approaching business problems and improving performance, using a coaching approach may yield the more expansive and creative results we've discussed. However, before the Leader Coach steps into personal and professional development, the parties must agree on proper boundaries that will be set and respected by both of them.

To begin, the Leader Coach needs to be invited in to certain aspects of the player's world and emotions. Next, the Leader Coach needs to truly consider whether to enter, even if invited. This is where the Leader must be cognizant of what issues are, and are not, appropriate for him to consider within the confines of the coaching relationship

One important consideration that is often times overlooked by both parties in their zeal to establish a meaningful relationship is that the Coach also maintains a responsibility to the organization. In the scope of this organizational responsibility, the Coach, when resuming his role as Manager/Leader, may have the task of completing a performance appraisal. In these instances, the Leader must assess performance in the harsh, real world, terms of whether a player gets to stay on the team or is asked to move on; whether he or she will be promoted, as well as setting the amount of a person's pay increase, which in itself can be a source of consternation for both participants. There will be certain players where it will be very prudent to set strong boundaries as to the extent and degree of the coaching relationship. In certain relationships both parties may feel very comfortable discussing emotions and how they impact behavior and results. Yet, in others, discussing emotions and value sets may be best served by leaving them totally off-limits.

So as to minimize problems from ever arising, it is extremely important that all of these types of concerns be addressed in the course of a frank discussion between the Leader Coach and Player at the very outset of the relationship. Just as it is possible for a parent to have different forms of relationships with each of their children, "loving them differently while loving them all the same," so too is it possible with a Leader Coach and his players. We hope it's a discussion and a relationship you approach with an open mind, an open heart, and a soul willing to be exposed. It will be a period of growth and exploration for you both, and most certainly a benefit for all concerned in the future.

Conclusion

Okay, some heavy stuff for the first chapter of what is intended to be a light hearted approach to an extremely important concept in Today's relationship-based world. One lesson that remains very clear in the lives of great leaders such as Abraham Lincoln and Theodore Roosevelt is that leadership is not something we turn on and off, or something that we leave at the office. It is a way of life. The higher the office held by the Leader Coach, the more important that he be a true Leader Coach all of the time, possessing those qualities of leadership that we will outline in the next few chapters.

To be a coach one has to be willing to be coached and to continue his own journey on the path of knowledge and growth. A Leader Coach has to be a servant leader, dedicated to serving those over whom he has stewardship. Their success becomes the Leader Coach's success, and is often a good barometer about his own value to the organization. A Leader Coach should be a leader of leaders, which is one manner in which the leader coach can exponentially reach more people and develop more disciples.

Chapter 2

Internal

We had settled in at our table at Starbuck's, and started our meeting about this chapter with a joke, which someone at the next table, who of course was decidedly not trying to listen to our conversation, was completely mystified by it as evidenced by the blank look on his face. The joke starts with, "did you hear about the college kid who was caught cheating on his metaphysical exam? Yeah, he was caught looking into the soul of the boy sitting next to him."

Taken out of context, this joke is neither funny, nor does it make sense. But, in this chapter we are going to delve into the meaning of soul, and the importance of doing just what the joke contends to be a crime, namely, looking into not only our own soul, but that of the follower or player whom we are attempting to coach.

Before we do this however, we have to define and clarify a couple of other terms that we encounter on a daily basis. We believe that nobody will disagree that in the course of our adult lives, we have all been bombarded by the terms 'manager,' 'leader,' and 'coach,' and been conditioned to believe that these terms can largely be used interchangeably. As will become clear, if it is not already, we vehemently disagree. More than just semantics, we attach significant difference to these terms and titles. To do anything else, would be tantamount to saying that a GEO, a Lexus, and a Hummer are all the same because they are all cars, and transport us from Point A to Point B. The terms 'manager,' 'leader,' and 'coach' are most certainly not interchangeable and have very distinct meanings, and ranges of responsibilities attached to each of them.

As we also noted earlier, there are countless books written on the subjects of management and leadership. As individuals and organizations we think nothing of shelling out big dollars for these books that purport to share 'secrets' of great leaders and managers such as Warren Bennis, Jack Welch, and Donald Trump. If one is so inclined, one can also spend thousands of dollars going to seminars and workshops on the topics of management and leadership as well and hear from Colin Powell, William Bennett, Rudy Giuliani, and Zig Ziglar. But if we seriously pause and reflect a moment, we quickly realize that most of the purported secrets and silver bullets are just time-tested truths about relationships and accountability between those who lead and those who follow.

That being said, how *does* the Leader call up the Coach from within himself? In essence, the same shift the Leader made from Manager to Leader, is the same shift the Leader must call upon to make the shift from Leader to Leader Coach. The main thrust attached to this momentous change is simply the shift of the leader's focus from self to others: from himself and his own needs to those of players he leads, and the filling of their needs.

We were sitting at our usual table at Starbuck's, filling up the back of finished manuscript pages, napkins, as well as the window [which drew a few stares], as we tried to reduce what we are trying to explain, to a simple diagram that we could use to depict our proposed model of coaching.

In chapter 1 we introduced the idea that Leaders must ensure they address the administrative requirements associated with their managerial role, and that this mastery provides the foundation required to becoming an effective Leader. In Figure 2.1 we model this in a manner that shows management mastery as the foundation of a pyramid.

Leader Coach Evolution Model

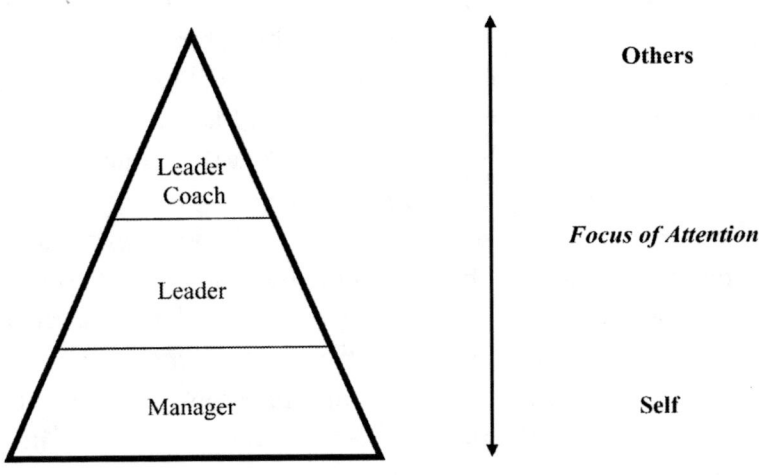

Figure 2.1

If you will recall, it is this mastery of management that permits the Manager to solidify his relationship with both the player and the organization that he supports. The Manager is the person who makes sure that quotas are met, efficiency reports written, and upper management receives the information that they need for the various and sundry reports that keeps Corporate America humming. It is also from this solid bedrock foundation that leaders are nurtured, developed, and grown.

Many of you may believe that you know of a large number of great leaders who are terrible managers, as evidenced by the fact that they don't take care of the basics, but, they can really motivate, or inspire a shared vision in front of an audience of two thousand associates. We both have worked for these charismatic, "the devil is in the details" sort of guys. While it may appear true on the surface that the basics are being ignored, we guarantee that the basics <u>are</u> being addressed, or have been mastered in the past, probably because the Leader has supported himself with an able administrator, or trusted second in command. It could also be that the Leader has delegated this responsibility masterfully to those he leads; but, either way we guarantee that these managerial basics are being addressed.

World renowned National Geographic photographer, DeWitt Jones, whose artwork and knack for capturing his subjects perfectly, claims that the key to his artistic ability is simply putting himself in the position for greatest opportunity (we'll talk more on this coaching technique later in Chapter 11.) But, Jones also claims that the foundation of all of his capability is a solid grounding in the requisite technical skills required to be *prepared* to win, or being *prepared* to capture an opportunity. So, before Jones, could get himself in the position for greatest opportunity, before he saw the magic he was looking for, he had to learn and master the nuances associated with film, film speed, f-stops, shutter speeds, and lighting techniques. After mastering these foundational techniques he was then able to take the next step up and place himself in a position to win and capture the opportunity.

Dr. Denis Waitley, one of our favorite authors on human performance, terms this foundation as L.U.C.K., or Laboring Under Correct Knowledge. Under Waitley's theory, it is those that prepare themselves to win, that find themselves to also be lucky. He believes that there are opportunities that present themselves daily to all of us, yet it is only those that have prepared themselves that are subsequently able to take advantage of these opportunities. Again, that's how we view this shift from Manager to Leader. When one has mastered the rudiments of managerial skills, then one is prepared to evolve into leadership. We certainly don't believe that people need to wait until they've completely mastered management before they step into leadership. In fact, if we were to more accurately depict the *Leadership Evolution Model,* we would depict it using Figure 2.2, where the boundaries between Manager, Leader, and Leader Coach are less distinct and more blurred, resembling the changing colors on a spectrum.

Leader Coach Evolution Model

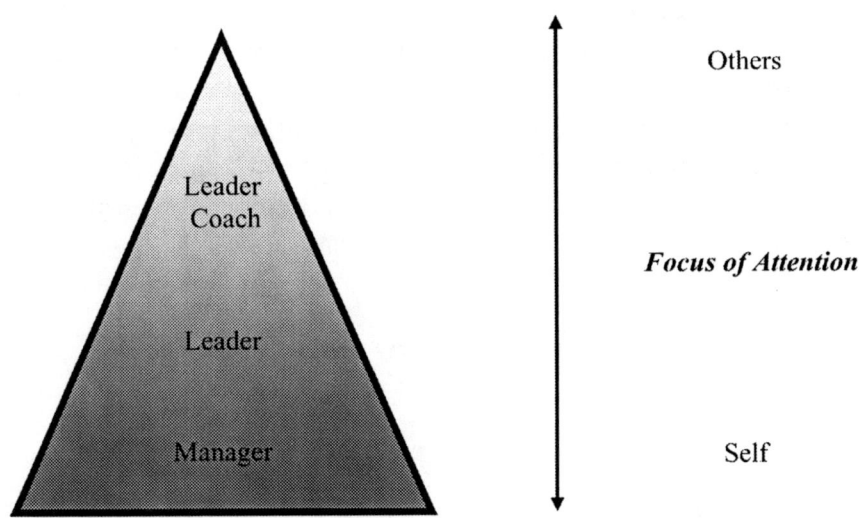

Figure 2.2

If we follow this logic through to complete the model, then we can see that it is through mastery of being a Leader, and the associated principles of leadership, that one then stands ready to step into the role of Leader Coach for another person.

We want to share one more word on this notion of the evolution of the Leader Coach competency. Dr. Neil Stroul[1], of Georgetown University's Leadership Coaching graduate certificate program, has developed a model supporting this idea of competency evolution. He has modeled a Learning Curve, which claims that once we've reached a point of mastery, we enter a state of learning known as "New Possibilities." This model is depicted in Figure 2.3. When overlaid with our *Leadership Evolution Model,* it depicts how managers initially focus on their own results or functions, then become masters of their domain, and then are prepared for "New Possibilities." Of course

---

[1] Neil is a Co-Director of Georgetown University's Leadership Coaching graduate certificate program and has been an Executive Coach to Terry.

this is cyclical, and actually resembles the three balls that make up your average snow man. Looking at our friend Frosty, we would see the larger bottom ball that serves as the foundation (management), which when completed provides a foundation for the second ball of leadership. Likewise, when this ball is firmly in place, we can add the third and crowning ball that represents the level of coaching. Once the skills associated with management are mastered, then the cycle begins again for leadership, and then later for that of the Leader Coach. We will examine more about "New Possibilities" in Chapter 11; for now, we are ready to continue our examination of the ascending relationship between manager, leader, and leader coach.

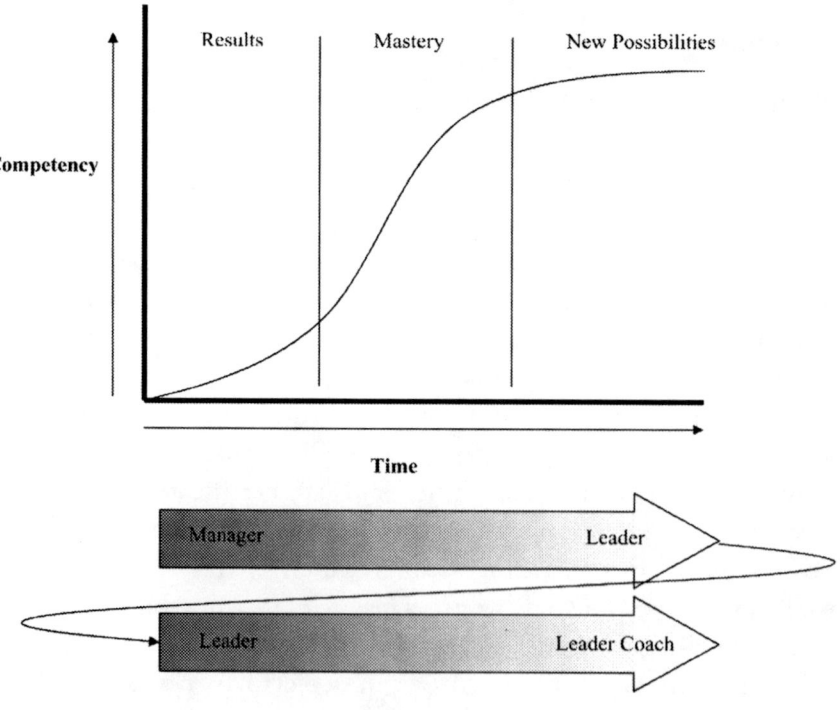

Figure 2.3

We know that some of you are still stuck on the concept that leadership is innate, and that one either is born a leader or is not. And, while we would agree that there are those that seem more predisposed to being great leaders than others, we also believe, as we mentioned in chapter 1 that we are all capable of becoming Leaders and Leader Coaches, if dedicated to our craft. We are all capable, to some degree, of compelling others to want to follow us, a set of corporate goals, or an inspired shared vision; naturally the success achieved will be a reflection of the other attributes and resources such as character and trust that the leader can muster. Thus, if we follow this logic, and the logic associated in developing the model in Figure 2.1, we are *all* capable of becoming Leader Coaches. It would then follow that that the only thing holding each of us back from becoming Leaders or Leader Coaches is our desire to do so.

What does it take to make this shift? We began to touch on it in chapter 1 when we defined leader coaching, and will amplify it in subsequent chapters when we talk about congruence, courage, heart, presence, and the willingness to take risks. For purposes of this chapter, we are talking about intent, bravery, acceptance of self and others, willingness to see the beauty in others, and naturally, the ability and willingness to expose our soul in this evolutionary process.

Too often Leaders/Managers are placed in positions of stewardship to others as a reward for the mastery of their technical skills. And, in this model, too often we end up losing our best technician (be it a programmer, forklift truck driver, or call center representative) and creating a mediocre leader. Too often organizations take this approach, and technicians are all too willing to try, because it is the only manner the organization has set up to financially reward and recognize their highly successful technicians, and it is the only avenue left available to the individual to advance. Unfortunately, without the intent to want to lead, we end up taking a talented player and putting him in a position for which he truly does not have an interest, and incent mediocrity. This is what has euphemistically been referred to as the Peter Principle, in which an individual 'rises' to his level of incompetence. We have all seen it, resisted it, protested it, but have largely been powerless to guard against it.

The other unfortunate outcome associated with this defective system of advancement is that it also invariably creates the perfect conditions for an individual to become a 'managerial lifer.' What is a managerial lifer? Simply, it is someone put in the position for all the wrong reasons, who will never excel in the manner he has in the past, and due to either technical expertise or acumen associated with the role, which he lacks, becomes frustrated. Over time, this frustration festers into something larger and uglier, until this individual becomes an often time angry, uncaring, apathetic manager.

This is a common issue in the military system where in order to achieve a twenty year career and earn eligibility for retirement an officer must be "well rounded" and be successful as both a commander and a staff officer to earn the requisite promotions and to survive the "up or out" syndrome. History is ripe with examples of great commanders who were terrible staff officers due to temperament and personality, as well as staff officers who were thrust into command positions with equally disastrous results.

The German Army on the other hand, has established two career tracts: one for commanders, and one for staff officers. This system attempts to maximize the skills and attributes of officers who are assigned to one or the other tract and remain there for the course of their careers. Naturally, there are limitations associated with this system as well, but the point to be made is that people are the most productive when they are challenged and satisfied in their work.

Returning to our discussion of the advancing technocrat, we view another less than satisfactory scenario, wherein this individual, through the use of 'smoke and mirrors,' remains highly successful, and continues to be promoted based on his ability to take care of the needs of his boss, or rides to success on the backs of his employees, leaving everyone befuddled and scratching their heads in amazement and wondering how this guy continues to get ahead. Neither of these scenarios is healthy for the organization as they are both breeding grounds for discontent and frustration on the part of the work force, as well as an inhibitor to real and sustainable growth, and is certainly a travesty and bastardization of the career path.

If it is not already apparent, it will readily become so, that we most certainly view the role of leading people as both a sacred responsibility and privilege that should not be abused. When a leader approaches and embraces this responsibility with this degree of reverence, only then will those for whom he has been granted stewardship feel the noble intent of the leader, embrace his character and example, and *desire* to follow him. This is as true of a leader of soldiers in combat, as it is a leader of a sales organization or manufacturer of widgets. This increased focus on others, rather than self, also is the main driving force behind the making of the Leader Coach.

Is it realistic to believe we can teach a manager to make this shift? Think of the managers you've encountered who may be accountable for hundreds of people, who can make the walk from their office to the bathroom, past dozens of people, seemingly with blinders on, and never even acknowledge one of them, much less call one of them by name. That's an extreme case, but how do we help them find the leader within? Think of the dynamic leader, whose people are drawn to want to follow him because of his charisma and vision, but who never slows down long enough to hear what his players are saying. How do we get him to love his people not only socially, but also for the talents and ideas that they can contribute – not just for their ability to follow through on his ideas, but more importantly for the discovery of new ideas of which he has never dreamed? These are the shifts we're speaking of in moving from Manager to Leader and from Leader to Leader Coach. How do we make this shift? We need to make an introspective shift in our thoughts and actions, and to really take a deep dive within ourselves, and to make our focus an internal one. We need to find and identify the very essence of our own souls, and to be in a position to proclaim to those around us just who we really are, and what we believe. From this appreciation of the essence of our basic self, we then have the confidence to want to find the souls, or the essence, of others with whom we work, and play, and love.

It is this appreciation of soul in both ourselves and others that we equate to "exposing the soul." Exposing the soul for us means discovering and then revealing, our souls to both ourselves as well as to others around us. We do so in an effort to garner the trust in those that we lead so that they too feel comfortable discovering and in turn exposing their own soul. When we live in the full presence and knowledge of who and what we are, our identities can easily be seen.

And, this willingness to be seen both invites and welcomes those we lead to approach us and to allow us to see them. It is within this comfort and revelry of our authentic selves and others that we are prepared to give up our egos and fully see the gifts of others. When we give up our egos and embrace our souls we have the freedom of allowing ourselves to not be right; the freedom to not be instructive, as well as the freedom to not direct. When we give up our egos and embrace our souls, we allow *others* to provide the right answers, to share their insights, as well as to determine how we are going to solve a problem. This is the approach of the true Leader Coach.

While we would love to think of the ideal leader as someone who is charismatic and has a wide following, the typical leader is unfortunately more commonly relying on the fact that he is calling the shots. The typical leader determines how difficult problems are going to be solved without input from those around him. The typical leader is directing the action. There are a number of reasons it works out this way. First, many times it is the leader that has the subject matter expertise to easily see what is wrong and how to fix it. Second, many times it is the leader that has been assigned this responsibility, and with our cultural norms, is expected to call the shots, not only by the organization, but also his subordinates. Third, many times the leader is the one at the "top of the heap" and simply believes that it is his prerogative to "call the shots."

The Leader Coach takes a different tack. Leader Coaches are great developers of people and most of our discussion in Chapters 9-11 will be about people development. But, the Leader Coach approach can also be used in directing the performance of an organization. The typical performance discussion about strategy development, or problem resolution, or performance improvement, is directed by the Leader or Manager. He generally has been the person in that position in the past and it is relatively easy for the Leader to quickly share expertise and insight and solve the issue. For many performance related issues this has worked extraordinarily well in the past. But, what do we miss with this approach? We miss a lot! When it is the leader that always solves the problems, then the organization develops a dependency on their leader that inhibits and retards growth of the individual and the organization. Both of us are parents (and yes even grandparents) many times over, in fact among the two of us there are 8 kids, and 7 grand kids – and we're both still relatively young. One of the things we pride ourselves on is the level of independence that our kids have developed for themselves with encouragement from us. We don't want to belittle any parent's approach, but we have noticed that in the families where the kids are non-stop calling out "Mom" or "Dad", that there is little independence being displayed. In these households, seemingly with every issue the child is experiencing, there's a need to call out for the caretaker. One of the many things we appreciate about our children, besides our close relationships and ability to effectively communicate, is the degree of independence our kids have in addressing their own issues. Beyond fostering independence, utilizing the Leader Coach approach can have a number of other advantages:

- **Diversity:** it allows for diversity of thought and alternative ways of finding all of the "right" answers. The Leader Coach approach necessarily provides for flexibility of thought and approach, which is the true value of diversity in the work place. All too often organizations and society measure diversity in the workforce by race or gender. We believe that diversity in the workforce should be a measure of flexibility. We've seen and been a part of too many companies that put a great deal of effort into diversity hiring, just to see diversity end there. People of diverse cultures and backgrounds arrive at an organization, simply to 'dead end' for two years and then move on, while those at the companies are left scratching their collective heads. What went wrong? The issue is that people of diverse backgrounds can approach work and problems differently. Without this acceptance of the soul, without the acceptance of the uniqueness and gifts of the individual, then there is never an appreciation for or a valuing of these diverse approaches and gifts. In essence there's only one way to be successful at the company.
- **Better ideas:** the leader or manager that solves problems strictly using his or her expertise is in fact limited to that set of experiences. By using a Leader Coach approach to problem solving, we allow the player to express his or

her own unique insights, and by doing so, we expand the approaches we take in solving problems.
- **Morale improvement:** nothing engages a player more than by being valued, and we believe nothing expresses are value for our players more than by asking for their help and input.

This Leader Coach approach is much different than mentoring. To further clarify, we would label what most leaders do as mentoring rather than coaching. As the saying goes, there's no substitute for experience. And, that's just what mentors share, their experience. The mentor assists the player by showing him the ropes, the way that he did things in the past, and attempts to enhance performance by sharing best practices. Please don't mistake this as criticism, we're both believers in the axiom, there's no substitute for experience. We just believe that mentoring and leadership can be enhanced by adding coaching to the equation. With this approach the player receives not only the benefits of our experience, but also the benefits of the experience and insight that he or she never knew was within themselves. The Leader Coach draws this out through the utilization of thought provoking questions.

The ultimate question each of us has to ask as a Leader or Leader Coach is "am I ready to be a coach?" As noted, the requirements are authenticity, consistency, and the desire to be the "real deal," beyond that of simply walking the walk and talking the talk.

The largest challenge for the coach is to refrain from the temptation of mentoring and providing the player with what we might view as the readily apparent answer, and assisting the player to discover this answer on his own.

CONCLUSION

This search for, and exposing of, soul doesn't come without work. Yet, when we uncover our souls it is as if there is an awakening from a deep sleep. The sense of peace that comes from answering the question, "who am I?" is exciting and freeing. But, the sense of peace that comes with answering this question also comes with obligation. The obligation is to help others, the obligation is to set aside self, the obligation is to serve, and the obligation is to make soulful connections with others. We use the word obligation to point to a service to others that comes from soulful presence, soulful leadership, and being a practicing Leader

Coach – Exposing the Soul. This is not an obligation of drudgery, but one of peace, comfort, and eternal reward. And, we guarantee that the reward and fulfillment associated with serving others is like nothing you have experienced before.

Part II

Foundation: Lessons in Leadership

In this part of the book we are going to focus entirely on the Leader and the attributes that are absolutely critical for him to possess in order to be effective. Having defined the Leader Coach as well as sharing the Leader Coach Evolution Model in Part I, we are now going to address the topics of *Congruence, Courage,* as well as present a *Model* that we believe captures the attributes of a true leader. While we do not purport that these three models or attributes are the least bit all inclusive of the skills requisite to be a highly successful Leader, they are representative of three models or values that we believe formulate the foundation upon which leadership, and ultimately leadership coaching are built.

It is our hope that this section will allow you the reader to become introspective, to conduct your own self-analysis, and to seek out assistance from your own coaches and mentors in any area that you may find yourself to be lacking.

Remember, coaching is not an event, it is a lifestyle.

CHAPTER 3

Congruence

One can only be a Leader, much less a Leader Coach, if one has achieved congruence in their own lives. Before you go rolling your eyes, and thinking that we are introducing yet another set of criteria for our Leader Coach, rest easy. By congruence, we mean a balanced professional life that reflects the five key tenets of the Leadership Congruence Model as advocated by James Kouzes and Barry Posner in their work *The Leadership Challenge*. This work is one that we would recommend to anyone interested in furthering their own abilities to lead others to success, and the attainment of stated and unstated goals.

As noted in the Preface, it is not our intent to present to the reader with a virtual tour of the various leadership theories currently abounding, but rather our own perspectives on what makes, or has made, a Leader successful in the leadership and development assistance that they can provide to those they lead. To this end, we have found that the very foundation that the Leader's own internal beliefs are built upon, are of paramount importance. Just as we know that we would not build a house on a base of sand, so too is it true that we have to personify the tenets of leadership to those whom we want to offer coaching.

Congruence as a leader means knowing the business inside and out, and possessing the ability to make decisions. It also means garnering loyalty as a two-way conduit, by earning it through the establishment, development, and nurturing of the proper environment. Sometimes this is a very modest undertaking, and may even go unnoticed. Other times it can be as brazen as the results achieved at the Pike Place Fish Market in Seattle, Washington, where employees and customers alike are treated to the high energy, fun seeking exploits of fishmongers doing their thing. Some of you may recognize it as the setting of the book and video series *Fish!* Other times, creating this environment may be very dramatic, and actually be about forging partnerships between employees, suppliers, and customers, much in the same manner as the country united after the dramatic and tragic events of September 11th. Many large companies literally opened their hearts and their corporate coffers that day, instilling great pride in their various constituents. In any event, it is the Leader Coach who creates this environment. The beauty of it is that no matter your level, whether you are the CEO, or simply a department manager wishing to take your department to a new level, you have the ability to do so *if* you yourself are in congruence.

Okay, you've been patient. We have danced around for an entire page, or four gulps of your Starbucks cappuccino. You are sitting there, maybe even fidgeting, and tossing pieces of your scone at the guy sitting at the next table, because you now have unanswered questions that are swirling around in your head. So what is *congruence*? How do I know if I have it? How do I acquire it? Does it *really* work, and is it habit forming?

Truth be told, the Leadership Congruence Model consists of five major components: Challenge the Process, Inspire a Shared Vision, Enable Others to Act, Model the Way, and Encourage the Heart. Each by itself represents a key component to the makeup of the true leader, and could be the subject of a work by itself. To this end, Kouzes and Posner offer *Encouraging the Heart*, an excellent working model that focuses on the importance of encouraging those whom we lead to always press on; to strive for excellence; and provides leaders with insights as to how they can have an impact through the art of influence.

CHALLENGING THE PROCESS

A review of the great leaders of the entire industrial revolution of the nineteenth, twentieth and early twenty first centuries would clearly make the point that leaders were, and are, pioneers, willing to take risks, to be innovative, and to experiment on both a limited and a grand scale. In this capacity, the Leader's primary contribution is to recognize good ideas, and as General Dwight Eisenhower was quick to demonstrate, not to denigrate the idea based on its originating source, even if it originated with a Private First Class. A leader's duties include finding the means necessary to support these ideas, and to formulate the strategy necessary to implement change and to demonstrate the willingness to challenge the status quo of the system and the process. Leaders who are truly successful at challenging the process are always part of the solution, and not simply part of the problem. They are problem solvers who learn more from their failures than their successes, and attempt to instill these same values in their subordinates. The true leader intent on challenging the process will keep one eye on the horizon with the long term perspective in mind, and one eye below the horizon so as to view the speed bumps that may be encountered and challenge the forward momentum of his team.

Theodore Roosevelt, from the time he was Police Commissioner of New York City, and most certainly while serving as our nation's 26th President, was all about challenging the process. Many of the reforms that we take for granted today are the result of TR's willingness to challenge the status quo and to raise the bar.

Learning and teaching were also vital parts of Roosevelt's leadership style. He learned by doing and by reading. A voracious reader, and one of the most prolific writers and adventure seekers ever to occupy the White House, Roosevelt believed that as a leader it was one of his responsibilities to educate his leaders. Decisive action, backed by intelligent forethought and decision making and the seizing of initiative when opportune, were the keys to his capacity for action, and his desire to challenge the process whenever he thought it was justifiable to do so. He attempted to instill this same desire in his subordinates. This is where 'thinking outside the box' is so important.

INSPIRE A SHARED VISION

There have been many great leaders of the past century who have had the ability to inspire a shared vision. Dr. Martin Luther King, Jr., in his famous *I Have a Dream* speech used artistry and graphic imagery to capture the hearts and minds of generations, and remains the classic example of artful communication being used to influence behavior. The speech that he delivered that day in August 1963 on the steps of the Lincoln Memorial was so masterful, so powerful, and incredibly impactful, because those listening to it were enthralled by the vividness of the images that he portrayed in terms of our country's majestic geography, as well as the concepts of people getting along with one another. While he delivered it without notes and appeared to be speaking extemporaneously, his efforts that day were actually the compilation of speeches that he had been practicing and delivering for months prior to that. Does that denigrate its impact, or the memory of it? No. It prevails in its beauty and power some forty five years later because it *was* a very powerful *vision* that served to *inspire* those listening to its creator, and largely remains the standard against which visions are compared.

Other examples of the last half century would also include President Franklin Roosevelt with his fireside chats leading a country of people full of desperation and despair, and desirous of hope, out of the Great Depression and then through the dark days of World War Two; Winston Churchill promising 'blood, toil, tears, and sweat' in an effort to lead Britain through its own darkest days as they fought on alone against Germany, and of course the Age of Camelot that began with John F. Kennedy's inaugural address where he challenged his countrymen not to ask what their country can do for them, but rather, what they could do for their country. Much has been written about the role of Kennedy's personal (and youthful) charisma having to do with the nation embracing his vision, as well as the impact it had on the televised debates he shared with then-Vice President Richard Nixon which influenced the outcome of the 1960 Presidential election. While charisma is something that definitely acts as a magnifier, what is remembered most from that period in history is the vision that JFK inspired with that single speech, and the manner in which it captured the hearts of an entire generation.

Clearly, leaders who are successful in inspiring a shared vision do so because they view things as they are, but also as they could be in the future. Robert Kennedy's "some men see things as they are, and say why, I dream of things that haven't been, and say why not," certainly illustrates this point. As leaders we are in fact, as Napoleon once expressed, "purveyors of hope." The Leader Coach takes this view, they dream, or help the player dream, of things that haven't been, and ask "what would it take you to make it happen?"

Leaders also have the ability to live their lives backwards. Like a chess player, they start with the desired end in sight, and work backwards to the present in an effort to first establish, and then achieve, the necessary milestones to effect change through inspiring a shared vision. It is our experience in a number of organizations that people actually thirst to be part of a vision that they can believe in.

So is this a new concept? Is this a New Age approach to leadership? Clearly, the answer is no. Historical precedent teaches us through the example of President Abraham Lincoln who expressed the thought that effective visions and organizational mission statements can't be *forced* upon the masses. Rather, they must be set into motion by means of *persuasion*. This is best done by first convincing the subordinate that you are his sincere friend, and then helping them readily adopt the vision as their own. To do this effectively, the leader must always be prepared to do the right thing, rather than doing things right, and integrity must be sincere. The topic of integrity will be addressed later in other chapters, but is a key component to subordinates buying into a leader's vision, and adopting it as their own.

Perhaps even more fundamental about inspiring a shared vision is Honest Abe's belief that "when you preach your vision, don't shoot too high. Aim lower and the common people will understand you." Likewise it is important to remember that when we are attempting to effect change through the adoption of a vision, that it is necessary to call on the past, transition it to the present, and to then project the past and the present together out into the future. This is a truth that Lincoln firmly believed in nearly 150 years ago, and remains just as true today.

ENABLE OTHERS TO ACT

While we often hear that it is "lonely at the top," and that leadership is all about making the tough call, much like it rested with General Eisenhower to "own it all" and to bear the brunt of responsibility for the success or potential failure of the Normandy invasion during WWII, true leadership is about creating the necessary environment in which leaders relinquish control to their subordinates, thus *enabling* them to act. As one mentor expressed it to one of the authors, "the more you give up, the more you get back."

Abraham Lincoln professed that when a leader "makes it to the top, [that] he should turn and reach down for the person behind him," thus empowering and growing the next generation of leadership. At the same time, Lincoln also believed in allowing subordinates to know that the honor would be all theirs if they succeed and the blame would be his if they fail.

One of the ways leaders "reach behind" is they never use the word "I", but rather, replace it with the word "we." This is a lesson that we have learned time and time again. Whether it is a sales organization looking for internal growth, or a military unit looking to consolidate on the objective, nothing serves better to the attainment of the end goal or mission accomplishment than the use of "we" and the sublimation of the leader's ego and self, thus enabling subordinates to act. Eisenhower masterfully did this by empowering his subordinate commanders to make as many decisions as possible at their various levels of command, but also by portraying the American Expeditionary Force's invasion and liberation of the European continent as a *crusade*. Use of powerful, inclusive, and emotional words such as crusade make people feel stronger, better about their abilities, and empowers them to act.

A word about the empowerment of subordinates, if you please. Empowerment can only be expected to come after subordinates are technically competent, are armed with goals that are specific, measurable, attainable, realistic, and time bound (SMART), and remains built on a relationship of trust and honesty with the leader. Without these qualities, people won't act, can't act, and most certainly will not feel inclined to do so if it involves taking risks. For without risk taking, there can be no change. Without change, organizations stagnate, and ultimately die. A common joke while one of the authors was employed by one of General Electric's companies, where change is literally and figuratively a constant, was that the last two letters of change are in fact, G E.

According to Lincoln, the ultimate test of whether you are a good leader is that "when your work is done, your aim fulfilled, your people will say, 'we did this ourselves.'" Enabling others to act, and to succeed, is the most powerful and tangible reward to coaching. Whether this is in the corporate environment or helping a youngster master the intricacies of riding a two-wheeler, it is all about the transference of knowledge, energy, and belief from the coach to the student.

Model The Way

The best sermon ever delivered is the one acted out rather than spoken. Much has been said that makes it imperative that a leader be able to walk the walk as well as talk the talk. By going first, setting the example, and defining the task, standards and conditions under which something is to be accomplished, *is* modeling the way.

Lincoln was a believer that a leader should "go out into the field with your leaders, and stand or fall with the battle." Patton, Bradley, and latter day Vietnam heroes such as Lieutenant General Hal Moore (the subject of the book and movie *We Were Soldiers Once…And Young*) and Colonel David Hackworth (*About Face*) certainly personified these tenets. Moore made the commitment to be the first man on, and the last man off, the battlefield, as his battalion was deployed. These leaders all were more than willing to demonstrate their leadership by sharing the hardships of their men, leading from the front, and being consistently clear in their guiding principles. Teddy Roosevelt demonstrated this while leading the Rough Riders in the Spanish American War of 1898. Roosevelt said: "no man has a right to ask or accept any service unless under changed conditions he would feel that he could keep his entire self-respect while rendering it." Other lessons from Roosevelt's example of leadership and service include knowing when to break the rules, and always striving to exemplify character. As a Leader Coach it is imperative that followers always observe an example worthy of emulation.

Encourage the Heart

Theodore Roosevelt offered that "words with me are instruments. I wish to impress upon the people to whom I talk the fact that I am sincere, that I mean exactly what I say, and that I stand for the things that are elemental in civilization."

Leaders always encourage those whom they lead to look for ways to be successful. Through their words, leaders have the ability to turn disaster into success. An example of this would be General Eisenhower's determination that there would be nothing but "cheerful faces at this conference table," while he and his key generals discussed options facing the Allies as they reacted to the Nazi offensive in the Ardennes, later known as the Battle of the Bulge. Eisenhower's desire to always buoy up those around him with optimism, allowed what could have been a devastating setback to the allied cause to become an overwhelming victory which broke the back of the Nazi war machine. This is also further evidence that even leaders need to have their hearts encouraged.

A classic example of leadership under fire where encouraging the heart was needed more than anything else, was the account of John F. Kennedy's leadership of the crew of PT109 after it had been rammed and sunk by a Japanese destroyer. While the movie may have glamorized the actual events, it still serves as a lasting example of a leader truly modeling the way, maintaining his own cool and determination, as well as encouraging the hearts of those around him. The accounts of Vietnam POWs and the role that Vice Admiral James Stockdale played in their survival by encouraging their hearts while captives of the North Vietnamese is another such tale of heroism.

Most of us won't have to endure the rigors of combat, or POW captivity, but will have the opportunity, on a *daily* basis, to influence the people around us. A good friend taught that there are "no small acts of kindness." A kind word on top of a successfully accomplished task may be of more value to the subordinate than any other form of reward. By the same token, a kind word to someone who is either frustrated, or having a bad day, may be the difference between life and death.

In this electronic age of cellular phone texting, blackberry messaging, e-mail, and standard form letters, nothing will provide the leader with the same powerful impact as that of a handwritten note. Followers will save them, display them, and view them as true fruits of their labors, even more so than cash bonuses, stock options, and other similar tangibles. Never underestimate the power of the pen being mightier than that of the sword.

Conclusion

The true Leader Coach serves as a model for how other leaders, as well as the members of their organization, can get extraordinary things done while battling limited resources, as well as constant change and other environmental challenges. By modeling the tenets of the Leadership Congruence Model, to include challenging the process when deemed necessary, a leader coach has the ability to inspire, encourage, and enable others to act within the bounds of a shared vision. Leaders lead, so others may act, and so that a common mission or goal can be attained.

Chapter 4

Courage

The dictionary defines courage as the "quality of mind or spirit that enables a person to face difficulty without fear." We believe that this definition is at best incomplete. While it portrays an ideal, it misses the mark. Yes, courage is an enabler, and potentially is the greatest quality of a leader. However, this definition of courage is also misleading in that it describes a person's ability to face difficulty *without* fear.

To believe that one can successfully face difficulty only without fear is both incorrect, and extremely misleading. Thinking that one can simply will fear to go away is nonsensical at best. It would be naïve to view courage in this manner. Our definition of courage would be the ability to face difficulty in the *presence* of fear. Leaders who can step in, especially in the presence of fear, and still have the where with all to take action – that is courage.

Another method in which we have addressed the subject of fear with our players, is to merely consider those pangs of fear as an awareness alarm that signals a lack of preparation. For experience has taught us that when we are prepared, we need not fear. This is a common lesson that we have taught all of our children in terms of preparation for school exams and the like. The Leader Coach assists his players in stepping into fear and taking action, or in other words: we encourage them to be better prepared, and to still function even in the face of fear that may have irrational origins.

Players in all organizations thirst for leaders around whom they can rally, and from whom they can draw confidence and sustenance in the form of their leader's courage. Lieutenant Audie Murphy was the most decorated soldier of World War II, and was a mere teenager of sixteen when he enlisted. Too small or too young for either the Marines or the Navy, he found himself serving as a common infantryman in the Army, the only branch of the services willing to accept him. His fearlessness, honor, integrity, and willingness to demonstrate exceptional personal courage time and time again, served to inspire those around him. It also earned him not only a battlefield commission, but a chest full of awards of bravery to include the Medal of Honor, the highest award for valor that can be bestowed upon a member of our Armed Forces. Perhaps more importantly, his personal conduct earned him the *respect* and *admiration* of his subordinates, peers, and superiors. Did Murphy feel fear? Did he question his own ability to lead? Of course he did. The difference is that he learned to master his fear, and to obviously utilize it as an asset to preserve his own life, as well as those of many of his followers. More often than not though, Murphy was driven to action by the events around him, and merely acted or reacted, rather than thinking about, or confronting, his fear.

Fear

Surprise, but fear is not a topic most of us want to talk about everyday. Even in some of the most intimate conversations we will have with our closest friends, few of us will be willing to directly answer the question, "What am I afraid of?" The inability to articulate an answer to this question is sourced from one of two places, either an *unawareness* of one's fears, or the *unwillingness* to admit one's fears. Let's be honest, fear is simply not something we want to admit to, or to talk about. If nothing else it certainly is neither cool, nor is it very manly. Exposing our vulnerabilities is not something that Society in general encourages us to do, much less the corporate world in which we all function. But, fear is a real presence for each of us in all parts of our life. We have fears about our relationships and our kids; we have fears about our status at work; we have fears about those with whom we work; we have fears about money; we worry about having enough money to maintain a comparable or better lifestyle in retirement; and like George Bailey of the holiday movie *It's A Wonderful Life*, we have fears about the value, or lack of value, we bring into the lives of those around us. These fears may not manifest themselves in either behaviors or reactions we would normally associate with the word fear or "being afraid." More readily, fear will manifest itself in a more subtle way, by subconsciously driving our emotions and behaviors. It is in these subtle ways that fear is given a more socially acceptable term for unproductive behaviors and emotions. Fear presents itself in emotions such as anger, anxiety, frustration, despair, disappointment, and jealousy. Fear can present itself in behaviors including rage, procrastination, suffering, unfocused activity, inaction, nervousness, indecision, false optimism, avoidance, and inattention. The successful Leader Coach does not succumb to these negative emotions or behaviors. Rather, he learns how to control and subdue them, and to ultimately use them as a tool. Ideally, he passes these techniques on to those whom he is coaching, thus improving their performance, enhancing their contributions to the team, and bettering their lives.

Fear as a Tool

It takes real emotional maturity to see fear as a tool, but that's just what leaders do. A Leader uses fear as a tool, and as a mechanism for extracting the very best from within them self, and when fortunate enough to pass this on to followers, to enable them to do so as well. The beauty of using fear as a tool, is that in the eye of the follower, the leader is in fact displaying a brand of courage that others want to emulate, albeit physical courage or moral courage. The ability to act is what sets them apart.

In the stories we tell about great leaders, many times we discuss them in terms of the decisions they have made or the actions they have taken. The actions our great leaders have taken in our stories include times when:

- **They've made difficult decisions** such as Eisenhower's decision to launch the D-Day invasion at Normandy during WWII. While Eisenhower recognized that the successful execution of this bold endeavor would have many willing to share in the credit, the onus of failure of this operation would rest solely on his shoulders. Despite this, and in light of changing weather patterns and the ability to additionally fortify defenses that a delay would afford the German forces, he made the decision to go forward. While he did not find himself under hostile fire as did Dick Winters and the other Easy Company soldiers, Ike's decision was one of the most momentous and courageous of the campaign.

- **They've taken unpopular actions and directions** such as Gerald Ford's pardon of his predecessor Richard Nixon. Clearly an unpopular decision that History with perfect hindsight has shown us to be absolutely in the best interests of the United States, as President Ford furthered the healing process, and avoided the spectacle of a former President of the United States facing felony charges and possible imprisonment.

- **They've tried something new** or to blaze new trails, such as the manner in which President Franklin Roosevelt closed the banks in order to reorganize them and to begin the stabilization and recovery of the U.S. economy. This was such a bold and unpopular decision that some of his closest advisors even questioned it. But in the face of adversity, and with a clear vision in his mind, FDR made the decision, and saw to its implementation.

- **They've engaged in difficult conversations** such as Harry Truman's decision to relieve General Douglas MacArthur as Commander of Forces in the Far East during the Korean War. An incredibly unpopular decision that his own advisors warned about the potential backlash from Congress as well as the general electorate. Tickertape parades, the ability to address Congress, as well as an intense public relations campaign by enemies of the President and supporters of MacArthur, did not cause this courageous leader to waiver in his determination.

- **They've shown their vulnerabilities** such as when Abraham Lincoln would humble himself or assume responsibility for the actions of his militarily incompetent generals, or write the mothers of fallen soldiers and express genuine remorse for their losses.

We talked earlier about Courage being the highest quality of great leaders. Doesn't it take courage to take all of the actions above? If a Leader is charismatic, insightful, or loving, it really means nothing unless those qualities are supported by action. Therefore, it is courage – the ability to take action in the face of fear – that truly let's a Leader's character shine like a beacon of light in the darkness. We believe that for Leaders to exhibit courage, they need to develop, possess, and master the ability to *be aware* of their fear, and the ability to *take action* in the face this fear.

COURAGE PERSONIFIED

Unknown to most who only knew to admire his athletic and adventurous adult life, Theodore Roosevelt actually grew up a sickly and frail young man. Much has been written about his ability to overcome a weak body by having a strong mind, and an indomitable spirit that like a fire burned brightly deep down into his soul. As a young man he came to embrace and personify the adage that courage is the first virtue, and lived his life in such a way that it became the very bedrock upon which all other virtues were built. His nearly obsessive body building, and adventure seeking, allowed him to reinvent himself, and to paint a canvas of moral and physical courage for others to admire and hopefully emulate. Roosevelt clearly believed that his example should be enough for others to develop their own internal pools of physical and moral courage, and a willingness to follow him under any circumstance. We could not agree more.

Likewise, Roosevelt believed that a leader who demonstrates courage under fire not only wraps himself in an aura of confidence that men will rush to in an effort to save themselves, but also generates confidence in the very endeavor of the organization, providing credence and strength to the vision.

Relating this to our own opportunities for displaying corporate courage as a Leader Coach, this means that our players will not only rally around us, deriving strength, but also an enhanced commitment around the corporate vision and goals that we promote to them. That is the value that a leader coach brings to the organization as well as to the players that he leads. Courage, properly demonstrated by a leader, conveys selflessness, character, and a leader's commitment to those he serves by leading them. One such act may produce incredible unforeseen results sometimes immediately, and in other cases, generations in the future.

AWARENESS

Fear is an incredible emotion that can drive some to despair, churning, and unproductive hiding. We've all arrived at points in our life where it feels like we don't know what to do next, either in a relationship or in a situation in either our personal or professional lives. In these moments we can become irritable, quiet, destructive to our selves, or prone to procrastination. It is in these times when the path forward might seem impossible to see and/or impossible to move towards. Yet, for others, true leaders, somehow they can use these moments as incredible internal motivators and become incredibly productive. These leaders are the ones who readily see *opportunities* where others might see events as *obstacles*.

Leaders feel the *presence* of fear and have the *awareness* to use it as their "early warning system". It is the awareness that he is in the state of fear that allows the Leader to look inward and determine that "something is not right". And, from the awareness of "something is not right" the leader begins the process of determining what corrective action must be taken so that things can be right.

How is this awareness developed? On the long running television show *Magnum P.I.,* our hero had a "little voice," that *talked* to him. For Terry, it was through the work with his own Executive Coach. Terry realized that when he wasn't achieving his desired results, he was not only frustrated with himself and others, but, he also seemed more irritated by his managers, disliked his position in life, and daydreamed of a change. He would catch himself thinking through situations again, and again, and again (stewing as we like to say) and while suffering through these "low times" in his career, was also prone to procrastination. His Coach helped him to see that when he procrastinated, or when he was simply beginning to worry, he could use it as a signal that "something's not right." He now uses it as an awareness tool.

For Don, well, it is sometimes merely the *fear* of failure itself that can affect him. Despite a lifetime of modest success, a childhood-instilled fear of not measuring up can sometimes cause an irrational fear to seize him. Despite successfully negotiating arduous examinations such as the Bar Exam to become an attorney, as well as NASD Securities licenses 7, 24, and 66, something as simple as a qualifying examination for an additional designation is enough to get him worrying about lightning striking, and his being branded a *failure*. But being *aware* of this fear, and being strong enough now to confront it and to *resist* it, has allowed Don to do things even as crazy as skydiving and being a passenger in a race car. Mastering a fear is a "high" in itself!

This is also probably a good time to distinguish between physical courage and moral courage. The courage that we see exhibited on the battlefield, such as Audie Murphy's exploits is obviously physical in nature. What we most often hear from these heroes is that they were "merely doing what needed to be done," or more accurately, they were only "trying to stay alive." It is our premise that physical courage is usually thrust upon us, as in the above example. Moral courage on the other hand, requires a deliberate, character-driven, call to action. It is most assuredly a *call to action that has to originate from within the character essence of the leader.*

So what can we do to unearth and subsequently address the fears and demons that we each possess? Executive Coaching is one method to help understand what fears challenge each of us in our respective lives. It's certainly a tool that the Leader Coach can use not only for himself, but also as the coach in helping his players. Not all great leaders have had coaches, but there has been some mechanism by which they have developed an awareness of their fears and overcome them. For some of them it has been associated with tragedy, others with mentoring, and for some, a life-altering event. For you it maybe feedback from a trusted friend, it may be found in meditation, prayer, or calmed self-examination, or an event or situation where you are forced outside your comfort zone. In any event, when we search our own souls, when we expose our souls like Dante, to our own curiosity, our fears will be uncovered, awareness will be developed, and courage can be called upon to move forward.

A Call to Action

Having the awareness that one is experiencing fear and ultimately doing something about it are two very different things. It takes a very "big" person to admit one's fear, and it takes an even "bigger" person to be able to take action in the presence of this fear.

One of our favorite Bill Murray movies is, "What about Bob?" [Note: Terry's only-- Don wants to shoot Bob on sight for most of the movie, and identifies with Richard Dreyfus in this regard. He does however enjoy Bill Murray in *Groundhog Day*, in which Don became a cutting room floor extra during filming in Woodstock, IL.] In this movie Bob (Bill Murray) is being treated for his psychoses by the therapist character played by Richard Dreyfus. One of the techniques used by Bob's therapist (in this moment, his coach) is encouraging him to "take baby steps" into his fears. The idea is that to take on the fear all in one fell swoop may be overwhelming and potentially defeating, but at least if a "baby step" is taken toward the fear, progress is being made. In one scene it was a fear of an elevator, and the productive step Bob took was to literally take "baby steps" toward the elevator. Not to diminish the role of the Leader (and Leader Coach) with the zany antics of Bill Murray or the trivia notes of the authors, it is important to note that leaders have developed the productive habit of being able to "take baby steps" (action) toward their fear, and in that way, productively overcoming them. This step into fear allows the Leader to have followers. It is through the example of the Leader that the follower is willing to try as well. And, it is through the encouragement of the Leader Coach that the player develops his own method to step into his fear.

Getting Started

We've all had the often time awkward or painful experience of giving a player difficult feedback. Regardless of one's level of experience, or level in the organization, it's never easy or fun. For the inexperienced leader, the first few times can be down right frightening. Yet, with proper preparation and coaching from our own leader, we are able to muster the courage to have the conversation. This is an example of a baby step into courage. From these first few experiences, Leaders and Leader Coaches have the ability to develop the capability to not only provide feedback, but also to have rich developmental conversations, the subject of which we will delve into deeply in chapter 11.

FEAR AND THE LEADER COACH

The Leader Coach is someone that, through his own leadership, has developed the ability to become aware of his fears and despite them, to step into action. He is also the coach of his players, and therefore needs to assist them step into the same space. Dr. Neil Stroul in his unique approach to coaching, would identify this as helping his client identify his or her own "Hero/Heroine in Retreat." This is the awareness piece of which we have been speaking. Who is your player and how does he behave when he is afraid? Let's not confuse this with failure. The sets of behavior we all exhibit when we're "in fear" have in the past served us well. There's a lot of achievement to be attained when we're motivated by fear. At the same time, there may also be behaviors and results that don't serve us well in our work roles or life roles when we are being motivated by fear.

It is in this space, if invited by our players, that we as Leader Coaches can help them self-identify their fears and some of the behaviors or emotions that may signal to them that they are in fear. How do we help? We can help them *observe* what's happening, by *playing back* what we observe, and offer alternatives through our coaching sessions. Through questioning and active listening we can playback their own observations for them. We can be *fully present* with them, making it safe for them to "expose their soul" by also exposing our own. In essence what we are attempting to do with our players is assist them to become aware of their fears and to then help the player put actions in place that will allow him to step into, and through, their zone of fear, thus encouraging them to be courageous.

THE LEADER'S ENEMY – EGO

Earlier, we acknowledged the notion of fear being something that most people are unwilling to discuss. Why? Because of the overpowering impact this fear has on our egos. Not to be discriminatory about age, but this is potentially one area where age, and accompanying maturity, is a benefit. In our tender, developing years, our egos are potentially at their most vulnerable and in their most fragile state. Youth, with all of its accompanying magic and power, can lead us to believe we can do anything and that we are infallible, if not darn right magnificent. Well, in short, we are all magnificent, and we are all wonderful creations of this beautiful world's life force – whatever each of us might call it. Yet, it's our egos that take us off track and somehow begins the process of "stack ranking" us, or comparing our magnificence to that of others. It is in this destructive, fearful space, when we begin to stack rank *ourselves* that we either take actions derived out of fear (to puff up our own magnificence and egos), or we defend ourselves from someone seemingly challenging our magnificence.

In the style of exposing the soul, the Leader has developed the ability to let go of his ego, and can appreciate in all of its unique quirkiness, himself and those he leads – truly appreciating each person's magnificence. Once firmly on course, and having mastered the ability to set aside ego, the leader can then step into the space of Leader Coach and work with his players to assist them on the same journey.

CALLING UP COURAGE

So, there's been a lot of theory and discussion in this chapter about an uncomfortable topic. And, for you trained psychologists out there, we are certain an equal amount of disagreement. But, this is how we see courage and its special place in the world of leadership and the empowerment of Leader Coaches. Just to make it real, we thought we'd discuss what we have observed, what we have used, and how we have coached people on our teams to use courage in their respective roles as leaders. Certainly, our belief that exhibiting courage, or the ability to act in the face of fear, is not unique. As FDR quoted in his first inaugural speech,

> *"So, first of all, let me assert my firm belief that the only thing we have to fear is fear itself—nameless, unreasoning, unjustified terror which paralyzes needed efforts to convert retreat into advance."*

Although we may not be called upon to lead a country out of a great financial Depression, or to lead the country in a world war, we *will* be called upon to lead and help our people lead during periods when we, like them, have to face our fears.

Delivering Feedback

Earlier, we referenced the sensitivity with which a Leader Coach may sometimes have to approach the difficult task of delivering feedback that will not necessarily be pleasing to the player. All of us that have been entrusted with the leadership of others will inevitably also carry the responsibility of delivering feedback.

There is no doubt that it is certainly a joy to do so when the person we are talking to is someone who is exceeding expectations; developing new and larger opportunities for themselves, and we can share, with great appreciation and enthusiasm, their contributions. On the flipside however, where the player is not meeting expectations, or when some "tough love" may be in order, it will be our duty to be the bearer of these bad tidings. Yet, it will be in those difficult feedback sessions where we truly "earn our bars," and help the player grow. For we surely learn more from our failures than from our successes.

Later, in chapter 11, as we discuss the mastering of developmental conversations, we will hopefully turn these difficult conversations into real value-added learning conversations for both the Leader Coach and the Player.

Making Decisions

Certainly in the role of leader, we are called upon to make decisions on a nearly constant basis. Many are rubber stamp decisions, with limited risk, obvious in their scope, or involve little controversy. Yet, there are some that don't seem like decisions, but will nonetheless require incredible courage. The less obvious decisions such as the adoption of a direction belonging to a superior might not present itself as a "decision" at all. It is in these moments when we need to expose our souls to ourselves, affirm our worth, step into our fear, make the tough call, and potentially express a contrary view.

Admitting Challenges

Similar in nature to the discussion on ego, one of the most difficult competencies to develop is the ability to "ask for help." In leaders, it means demonstrating or exposing our vulnerability. But, it can be an incredible tool with which to engage peers, superiors, and your players. Who can resist someone who comes to you and validates your talents and expertise by asking, "Can you help me with something?" What a great way to show appreciation for someone's magnificence.

We as Leader Coaches should ensure we make space and create an environment in which our players can feel comfortable to ask for help, and feel that we do appreciate their courage in stepping into this space.

Being Bold

In the given examples above, advocating a new direction, or challenging the process, often in the face of contrary thinking, will most assuredly expose the leader to potential criticism. In order to achieve a bold new direction, it is necessary that the Leader Coach approaches the process with affirmation of self-worth, the utilization of logical analysis and a display of courage. This is what allowed many of our nation's historical figures to do the things that have shaped our collective history.

Conclusion

In terms of the leader as coach, it is critical that he displays all the attributes of courage. Going back to Kouzes and Posner's extensive survey of followers on the desired attributes in their leaders, we recall that Trust was first and foremost the most sought-after trait. Following trust, they include Competency, Forward-looking, and Inspiring. If we but pause for a moment and reflect on those leaders with whom we have worked and respected, or the coaches from whom we have learned and received inspiration, it becomes readily apparent that they embodied all of these attributes as well as that of being courageous. If we consider the leader as coach, it becomes even more apparent that for the relationship to be successful, the follower must have confidence in the leader, and believe that the leader possesses the courage to always seek the right path for himself, for the player, and for the organization, as well as possessing, and demonstrating a desire to expose his soul in an effort to nurture the development of the follower. In the absence of an ongoing and lasting relationship, coaching as a paid consultant is difficult enough. This is why coaching as a leader, dedicated to serving the interests of the organization as well as the individual, is an incredibly difficult undertaking. But for the leader who is willing to expose his soul, and invest his heart, it can be one of the most rewarding works ever performed. We readily do it with our children, seemingly without thought; and yet when it comes to doing it in the workplace it often becomes a challenge. The key to success is to truly *love* those whom we serve, and to employ all the traits of a servant leader when assuming the mantel of Leader Coach.

Theodore Roosevelt personified all of these tenets. Rising above a sickly and frail body, with an indomitable spirit, and thirst for knowledge, and to impart it to those around him, he led his life in such a manner as to personify courage as the first virtue.

Players in all organizations thirst for leaders around whom they can rally, and find confidence and sustenance, especially in a world that is ever changing. Again, our own opportunities for displaying corporate courage as a leader coach will come when least expected. In order to insure that our players will not only rally around us, but also around the corporate vision and goals that we promote to them, we have to model the way, and rely on our courage. That is the value that a Leader Coach brings to the organization as well as to the players that he leads.

CHAPTER 5

Modeling

We believe that the largest single component of the leader is his character, or in other words, his soul. By soul we mean the very essence of the leader. Does he possess the attributes necessary to command the respect of his followers? What these attributes actually are, have been the subject of countless leadership, management, and psychology books. As a retired career military officer, and having observed the military leadership "up close and personal," for over thirty years, one of the authors believes that the U.S. Army's Model of Leadership presents a concise summation of the necessary traits of soul, known simply as Be, Know, Do.

THE ARMY MODEL OF LEADERSHIP: BE, KNOW, DO

Much has been written about the 'best damn ship in the Navy way of leadership' or the 'Marine Corps approach to leadership,' and with the popularity of the *Rambo* and special services movies, countless volumes about "Ranger leadership" and "No excuse" leadership, this proliferation continues with no end in sight. Fundamentally, all of these have a common core set of skills that can be found in the tenets of U.S. Army Leadership, which itself is based on courage and the willingness to act. In true institutional fashion, the leaders of the United States Army have attempted to distill these principles into a Field Manual, or "FM", aptly entitled, *Field Manual 22-100: the U.S. Army Leadership*

Field Manual. One quickly notes that originality and marketing are not a high priority to the development and distribution of these materials.

With over 230 years of experience, the United States Army has had much written about it. It has been described by some as one of the most complex, best run organizations, and at the same time by others as an oxymoron in terms of 'military' and 'intelligence.' However, like the corporate conglomerate General Electric, it enjoys a long and storied history of producing exceptional leaders. The United States Military Academy at West Point has produced some of history's greatest leaders of the past two centuries: Generals Ulysses S. Grant, Robert E. Lee, Douglas A. MacArthur, George S. Patton Jr., Omar N. Bradley, Dwight D. Eisenhower, and H. Norman Schwarzkopf, just to name a few. State institutions such as the Virginia Military Institute have produced leaders such as George C. Marshall, and the Reserve Officer Training Corps (ROTC) has given the Army, and this country, men of stature such as Colin L. Powell. While their paths into the Army may have varied over time, all have been subject to mentoring and strong leadership development.

The key to the Army model of leadership, hereinafter *Be, Know, Do*, has been the concept of dispersed leadership in which leaders are taught and nurtured in ways to inspire and lead the men and women over whom they are charged to provide command. Inherent to the success of the organization is the fact that every member of the chain of command has the ability and willingness to step up and to fill the void as leaders are killed, incapacitated, or promoted upwards. Key to this leadership development is innovative training and the [obvious] vertical promotion from within its own ranks. Audie Murphy's rise from rifleman to squad leader to platoon sergeant to that of platoon leader, or Dick Winters' rise from platoon leader to company commander and battalion commander as portrayed in *Band of Brothers* is evidence of this principle at work.

Leadership has very clearly been the difference between success and failure in the military for as long as man has formed armies and gone to war. A clear chain of command, from the King or Emperor or Commander-in-Chief down to the rifleman in the infantry squad or the tank driver, is what allows complex missions to be broken down to individual assignments that can be executed to successful outcomes.

Everyone who wears a uniform does so with pride and with a sense of belonging to an organization that is larger than any one of them. Those who 'wear the green' do so with conviction, and the willingness to do more than simply follow orders of those appointed over them. Terms like 'Mission First, People Always' reflects the commitment of the individual and the leader to the overall goal, as well as the leader's [at all levels] desire to serve and strengthen the individual so as to promulgate the successful completion of the mission. It requires a *desire*, on the part of everyone involved, to accomplish the mission by any means possible. For the leader it should be a desire to *influence* his subordinates by inspiring a shared vision, providing direction and motivation, all the while using persuasion rather than raw authority to create the impetus for action.

According to *Army Leadership*, "leadership transforms human potential into effective performance." Amidst all of the stated objectives of any organization, it is clear that this is something that every organization should have as its primary goal for its most valued resource: its people.

It should also be noted that every leader is also a follower, and this is true at every level, regardless of rank or organizational assignment. Inherent to effective leadership are three components which the Army has refined to three words: *Be, Know, Do.*

BE

Just as the "fish rots from the head down," leadership begins with the person at the top. More importantly, it starts with the *character* of the leader, and the manner in which he conducts himself. Character comes from *within* the leader and is reflective of the values and attributes, as well as the courage that determines the actions of the leader. Consistency of thought and deed, is critical to a leader achieving success with his team, regardless of size. Again, we cite the results compiled by Kouzes and Posner in their classic work, *The Leadership Challenge,* in which thousands of people across a wide array of businesses and organizations ranked trust and honesty as the attributes that they most looked for, and valued, in their leaders. No other attribute was deemed as important as Trust. When it is present, anything is possible. In its absence, very little is possible. If we pause, and consider those leaders for whom we have worked in our own lives, we would have to recognize that the presence or absence of trust more often than not determined our relationship with this leader, our attitude toward the organization, as well as whether we were jointly successful in achieving organizational objectives.

The qualities of trust and honestly can only be demonstrated by consistency of both word and deed. Remaining calm under fire and reacting in a consistent manner regardless of the depth and breadth of the problem being presented is what inspires confidence in the subordinate.

Character can also be used to describe the Leader's True North. Despite the reading of the compass due to outside distractions and influences, a leader's True North does not change. These are the very attributes that reflect who a person is and will be. This is demonstrated not only during crises in command, but in day to day activity. Honor, integrity, and duty are best portrayed in actions rather than words. The best sermon is the one that is acted out rather than delivered.

The core values of the Army's *Be* form the acronym LDRSHIP.

> **L**oyalty
>
> **D**uty
>
> **R**espect
>
> **S**elfless Service
>
> **H**onor
>
> **I**ntegrity
>
> **P**ersonal Courage

Sociology tells us that values are instilled in leaders as children by their parents, and that we "are" the person we are going to be largely by the age of ten. This being said, we must also consider that leaders, like values, are largely who and what they are going to be by this age, and are subject to being refined by environment. "Do as I say, not as I do," obviously has no place in defining the character of our leaders. Our subordinates rightfully demand that their leaders walk the walk while talking the talk.

KNOW

In addition to *being* a leader of character, leaders have to *know* their craft. They have to possess interpersonal, conceptual, technical, and tactical skills requisite to the organization that they are leading, and attempting to instill the attributes of, through coaching, in their subordinates. Whereas the character attributes of *Be* probably have to already exist within the individual when they join the Army or any organization for that matter, those associated with *Know* can be learned or acquired through training, education, and awareness.

Interpersonal skills range from the art of the basics of communicating, smiling, caring, mentoring, teaching, counseling, to that of coaching, motivating, empowering and developing individuals, as well as inspiring a shared vision and team building. Obviously an individual's personality, e.g. extroverted v. introverted, has an impact on his interpersonal skills, but a good bit of these more mechanical skills can be learned or acquired with effort and appropriate training.

Conceptual skills include the ability to think strategically or globally or in other words, to view the big picture, as well as to look several moves ahead as does a chess player while engaged in combat on the game board. Whether the ability to think creatively and to apply critical and analytical reason to any given situation or problem is either an inherent skill or one that can be acquired through training and practice is subject to debate, and is clearly beyond the scope of this writing. In any event, the ability to reason analytically and to apply the ethics of the organization to any given situation forms what followers look for in a leader's judgment. Followers want to know that they can rely on their leaders to be honest, consistent, and to reach decisions based on a foundation of historically sound judgment. The calming influence of a leader such as Captain Dick Winters in the chronicles of Easy Company in *Band of Brothers*, could not more graphically illustrate the importance of this attribute.

Technical skills are the skills inherent and necessary to performing successfully in the role being occupied by the leader and the follower. This is when the leader who has worked his way up through the organization has a decided advantage over the outsider. Experience and the opportunity to have walked in the shoes of the follower enhance the leader's credibility, and reinforces the follower's desire to accept direction from the leader. As a Leader Coach, this takes on even greater significance, whereas an Executive Coach has greater leeway in that technical skills may or may not have any bearing on the coaching relationship.

Tactical skills by simple definition are the complement to conceptual skills. In the Army they may revolve around skills necessary to achieve success on the battlefield ranging from the achievement of mass and surprise while conducting an attack as employed by General Patton while he led Third Army on a swath through France into Germany to more subtle, basic soldiering skills necessary to survive. For those of us fighting with boardroom roles, these skills could include the art of negotiating, resource allocation, as well as the preparation of short- and long-term budgets, plans, and calendars, as well as succession planning.

In any event, the leader has to *know*, or be proficient in, a wide range of skills while possessing the necessary traits of character. The absence of either of these skills (*Know*) or character (*Be*), will most decidedly inhibit the success of the leader and the organization.

DO

When discussing *Be* and *Know* we are inherently discussing all the inner workings of a successful leader, or more succinctly those attributes and skill sets that the leader is either "born with," had instilled as a child, or developed while rising through the ranks that leads to his current position. Again, the best sermon is the one that is delivered by deeds rather than words. In terms of Army leadership, General Patton made it clear to his subordinate commanders, that "in cold weather, General Officers must be careful not to appear to dress more warmly than their men." In the corporate world, this may be interpreted that leaders are prepared to act, and to *do*. The leader that truly uses influence to motivate the behavior and productivity of his subordinates is also the leader who is both *willing* and *able* to roll up his sleeves and to work along side his followers. Whether it is joining the assembly line for part of a shift, or driving a forklift, it is the ability to do so with the proper heart and character that inspires confidence, and encourages mission accomplishment. By displaying the requisite knowledge, and the desire to achieve the mission by always keeping one eye well above the horizon looking forward, with the other eye directly in front of the team, seeking out obstacles and finding solutions, he will inspire his players to want to follow.

Conclusion

In terms of the leader as coach, it is critical that he displays all the attributes of *Be, Know,* and *Do.* Going back to Kouzes and Posner's extensive survey of followers on the desired attributes in their leaders, we recall that Trust was first and foremost the most sought after trait. Following trust, they include Competency, Forward-looking, and Inspiring. If we but pause for a moment and reflect on those leaders with whom we have worked and respected, or the coaches from whom we have learned and received inspiration, it becomes readily apparent that they embodied all of these attributes. If we consider the leader as coach, it becomes even more apparent that for the relationship to be successful, the follower must have confidence in the leader, and believe that the leader possesses the attributes of Be, Know, and Do, as well as a desire to expose his soul in an effort to nurture the development of the follower. As previously noted, coaching as a paid consultant is difficult enough; coaching as a leader, dedicated to serving the interests of the organization as well as the individual is an incredibly difficult undertaking, and not for the faint of heart. But for the leader who is willing to expose his soul, and invest his heart, it can be one of the most rewarding works ever performed. We readily do it with our children, seemingly without thought; and yet when it comes to doing it in the workplace it often becomes a challenge. The key to success is to truly *love* those whom we serve, and to employ all the traits of a servant leader when assuming the mantel of Leader Coach.

Heart, and soul, properly demonstrated by a leader, conveys selflessness, character, and a leader's commitment to those he serves by leading them. One act may produce incredible unforeseen results.

PART III

*Preparation:
Personal Attributes of a Leader Coach*

Before we get into the heart of the Leader Coach-Player relationship, and the three levels of conversations that the Leader Coach must master, we will first complete our survey of what attributes the Leader Coach must bring to the relationship. For that is what leader coaching is all about: a relationship. It is absolutely imperative that a very firm relationship be established, nourished, *and continue to grow* during the leader coaching relationship. Whereas the Executive Coach plays a critical role in a player's development from outside an organization, the Leader Coach is on the field with the players, and has multi-faceted relationships and a significantly higher investment.

It is our hope that this section's chapters, entitled *Heart, Presence,* and *Risk,* allows you the reader to become further introspective, and to conduct your own self-analysis, as well as begin to examine the basis of the relationship between you and your player(s).

Again, coaching is not an event; it is a lifestyle which we must embrace with vigor.

Chapter 6

Heart

We believe that we have probably already made the point that being a Leader Coach is far from an easy task, and that a good bit of a Leader Coach's success will be dependent upon the degree that he invests and leads with both his heart and soul. So far we have talked about the importance attached to a Leader Coach being willing to expose his soul, and the necessary willingness to address his own fears, and risk the potential disappointment and accompanying pain of failing to help a follower maximize their potential. Now we want to delve a little deeper and acknowledge that it is important that the Leader Coach also be willing to invest a good bit of his heart, as well as to display this heart by both word and deed.

By heart, we mean that the Leader Coach has to be courageous, trustworthy, command the respect and loyalty of his followers through a process of reciprocity, and to truly be a servant leader. While we will define servant leadership in greater detail later, for now it means that he has to love his people, and to be willing to expose heart and soul, and to risk being hurt in the process of doing so. He must desire the best for his team and its members, and most important of all, derive satisfaction from the very act of coaching.

SERVANT LEADER

What does it mean to be a servant leader? We believe that a servant leader is in fact a leader who is committed to the success of those he leads. By dedicating his efforts to the success of his subordinates, and finding genuine joy in their growth and advancement, his leadership efforts truly become selfless gestures, and benefit not only the individual receiving the coaching, but also the organization, as well as the coach himself. These efforts will come naturally if the leader coach in fact *loves* those he is leading, and cares about them as individuals and as an integral part of his organization.

LOVE IS...

Coach Vince Lombardi recognized that love has a very large and very real place in every organization. In his words, "I don't necessarily have to like my players and associates but as the leader I must love them. Love is loyalty, love is teamwork. Love respects the dignity of the individual. This is the strength of any organization."

LOVE AS A VERB

What did Lombardi mean when he used the word *love* as he did? James C. Hunter, in *The Servant*, referenced the Greek word for love or *philos*, or brotherly, reciprocal love. This is identifiable as the 'you do good by me and I'll do good by you' kind of conditional love. This root word later gave rise to the name of the City of Philadelphia, otherwise known as the city of brotherly love, [except when the Dallas Cowboys play the Eagles.] The more commonly used word to describe the type of love that we are referring to here, comes from another Greek word *agape*, and the corresponding verb *agapao*, which refers to a more unconditional love which is rooted in behavior, in this case on the part of the coach, with no regard for any form of quid pro quo. It is purely the choice of the coach to emulate the form of New Testament love that Jesus spoke of to his disciples. The Golden Rule also has its foundation in this form of behavior based on choice rather than feeling. In other words, and to refer back to Coach Lombardi, regardless of how the coach *feels* about the player, it is incumbent upon the coach to unconditionally *behave* in a proper manner towards this person. Much as being the parent means retaining self control and not "stooping to the level of behavior" that a misbehaving child or teenager may be displaying, so too must the coach always be in a position of modeling the way, and not violating the tenets of character that the rest of the team may be relying upon for their own development. As Leader Coaches, we will both freely admit that this can be very difficult when dealing with one particular team member who is recalcitrant in his or her attitude, may act to undermine you, and is otherwise a disruptive influence on the team. That is when you will be tested as a Leader Coach. It is our hope that if this work helps you in just one way to achieve any of your goals that you will share it with another coach.

Heart and Hurt

Inherent to the entire coaching relationship is the willingness on the part of the Leader Coach to not only devote himself and his best efforts to the success of his players, but also a willingness to care enough to *risk* being hurt in the relationship. In the example that we just referenced where you may be dealing with a player who is recalcitrant or even undermining your efforts, it is very hurtful, because you are exposing your heart and soul, and basically having it walked on and kicked aside. It is in these moments that a Leader Coach could be tempted to abuse the authority of his office, and to come down really hard on the player. This again, is the real test of leadership and coaching. We wanted to make this point perfectly clear, because to believe that coaching is purely a positive experience, free of heartbreak or at a minimum, disappointment, would be naïve. The good news is that since coaching is based in relationships, and largely done on a one on one basis, these disappointments and frustrations can be contained, and dealt with in a manner that they don't disrupt the greater balance of your efforts.

Desire the Best for the Team

The Leader Coach is selfless in his desire to see the individual members of the team, as well as the team as a whole, achieve a level of success not previously attained. While he himself may be a beneficiary of this individual and team success, the main focus of his efforts must be in the raising up and success of these individuals. We are not suggesting that to be an effective leader coach that an individual has to take a vow of poverty and renounce all earthly possessions and forego his own career ambitions, but rather he needs to maintain a careful balance between his own needs and ambitions and those of his team members. These goals can be mutual, and simultaneously pursued, if a leader maintains a proper level of congruence in his life, and also finds joy and self-actualization through these coaching efforts.

Self Actualization

Self-actualization can only be achieved after all of our other basic needs, e.g. social, love, affiliation, and egoistic, have been met. By definition, self-actualization needs are those motives and/or actions that are set into motion in order to fulfill an individual's form of soul. Or as Frank Sinatra would have said it in song, "I did it my way." The beauty of achieving self-actualization as a Leader Coach through the act of coaching stems from the fact that it is reflective of the selfless service spoken of by the Savior, and reflects a desire to seek and promote good in those around us. Aside from our experiences as parents, there has been no greater joy, or level of success we have enjoyed more than watching those whom we are coaching discover new or enlarged talents, and achieving their own brand of success.

Leadership and Heart

Is there a connection between strong effective leadership and heart? We believe that there most assuredly is a very distinct correlation. Up until now we have defined the coach, emphasized the internal component of the coach within, examined the necessity of the Leader Coach being in congruence, and exhibiting true courage, as well as modeling his craft by the Army Model of Be, Know, Do. But the name of the book mentions soul. So what about soul?

Soul

So what about soul you say. Our souls and the souls of our fellow leaders are the very foundation upon which great leaders, and people for that matter, are built. It is only after we have matured enough to expose our souls to ourselves and to others that we become capable of leading from the heart, being in congruence, and shedding or setting aside our egos to be of service and available for others.

To come to a true understanding of our souls takes some genuine work as well as general living. For it is only through experiencing life that we understand the pain and destruction of living a soulless life. It is also through experiencing life that we understand the challenges and seductions of a life centered on self and not on soul. When we center on self we are drawn away from our authenticity and beauty. What forces draw us to self and away from soul? The forces of status, greed, lust, insecurity, and shame are just a few. As we'll mention in Chapter 9, it is difficult in Today's corporate environment not to be drawn to self. For the very structures and rewards meant as incentives to executives and manage their time are the very structures that are incentives to greed, lust of wealth and power, and status. Again, we don't want to lead you to believe that we are Altruists or that we don't look forward to the rewards of being a leader; yet, it is when we measure our worth by these symbols that the leader's insecurities become too great to be of much use to the people being led. What we do believe though, is that for a leader to progress to the level of Leader Coach requires "soulfulness." As we discussed in Chapter 4, to develop and exhibit the leadership trait of courage requires a degree of confidence that we believe only comes from a loving, confident soul.

It is from this strength of valuing ourselves and our souls that we can then value and love the souls of others. In this state of soulful confidence we see each soul as having its own uniqueness and beauty, each a masterpiece of creation, and each worthy of respect. This does not mean that every soul or person will be right for our organization. As we discussed in Chapters 2 and 5, it is a requirement to possess the base level technical skills of one's role in order to achieve expected results and mastery, before we step into leader coaching for New Possibilities. Nor does it mean that our souls and the souls of others are without fault or quirkiness, quite the opposite, we all have our peculiarities. But, it is the ability to be soulfully centered and respectful of each person's soul, in all its greatness and even weirdness, that is a distinction of the Leader Coach. As Thomas Moore states in his book, *Care of the Soul*, too often we are encouraged in today's society to exorcise or ignore our soulful peculiarities and hurts. Yet, he believes that it is through acceptance of our entirety, through acceptance of our whole soul, even the bizarre stuff, that we develop the ability to accept our full being and that of others. As we'll discuss in later chapters, we also believe this acceptance is the basis for diversity within our organizations. In our soulful model of diversity we see diversity as being far more than the mere acceptance of different colors, genders, or sexual preferences; and, more being the acceptance of diverse souls.

In our opinion, the focus on the soulful or spiritual or authentic leader will be the next break through in leadership. A look back reveals that the 80's was the decade of quality and the 90's was the decade of change leadership. These decades also ushered in the disregard for loyalty and commitment between employer and employee, and the decline of morale and loyalty which has created an environment in which the average employee feels like nothing more than a contract player. Coupled with the resurgence of the industrial revolution-like reward structure of a dollar paid for a dollar worked, no more no less; and, the devaluing of institutional knowledge as witnessed in the waves of layoffs and mergers, how are leaders to engage and *retain* talented players? We will engage our talented players through soulful connections, made possible by exposing our souls and *valuing* the souls of those we lead. Through soulful connection, we will not only engage our players, but we will also be *available* for them and focused on their needs and development. With this heightened focus of attention on them, we will grow from leader to leader coach; and, we will develop a unique brand of loyalty based on relationships and commitment to personal growth.

STAYING SOULFUL

Staying in this centered space of soulfulness is all well and good, but realistically neither of us has cracked the code of being fully, soulfully present all the time. It's just too darned hard with full schedules, crowded spaces, incessant noise, and exposure to uncivil behavior that seems all too pervasive these days, to remain quiet-minded and fully available for ourselves and others. Unfortunately, when we step away from being soulfully present we actually become fearfully present. When we're fearfully present, the destructive fear-based behaviors we discussed in Chapter 4 come bursting through. These behaviors, if you'll recall, included abruptness, rage, and in particular reference to the absence of soulfulness, impatience. Just as we claimed in Chapter 4 that ego was the enemy of the leader, we believe that impatience and the frenetic, inefficient energy that accompanies it, is the enemy of soulful presence. In the state of impatience, our thoughts become less rational, our fears of poor performance are heightened, our capacity to reason is diminished, and we are less able to work in partnership with, much less coach, others.

How do we remain soulfully present? We intentionally create an environment around us that enables us to be more likely to live in this space. For each of us, creating the environment that is most conducive for us to be quiet-minded and soulfully present will differ. Some things that have worked for us include:

- **Time management:** We need to be intentional and protective of our time. If we find ourselves running from engagement to engagement with little to no down time or thinking time, there's not a lot of opportunity to re-center or get soulful; in fact, it would seem that the more intense and inflexible our schedules become the greater the possibility for impatience and fearful presence (the opposite of what we're trying to achieve).
- **Hobbies that foster peace and happiness:** For each of us these activities might vary as wide as our personality types, ranging from basket weaving to free style rock climbing to golf. The point is to engage in a non-work activity that brings joy and contentment.
- **Be selective about the company you keep:** The idea behind living soulfully is living intentionally. For when we live soulfully we're living the life we want and intend to lead. The unfortunate byproduct of a life lived unintentionally for us is a group of friends and acquaintances that do not support our intentions. We need to consider what activities allow us to live and be ourselves and who we want to be and whether these previous friends and acquaintances support or detract for our ability to live this intention.

- **Soulful habits:** Again the habits that connect us with our souls can vary widely. Some that we have found very useful include exercise, prayer, meditation, massage therapy, yoga, and journaling. Among the more contemplative activities of prayer, meditation, and journaling, we would recommend getting very intentional about the uncovering of one's soul, essence, fears, and emotions. Our goal is to develop an ever-greater awareness of who we are, what we love, and what brings us joy and contentment. With this heightened awareness we can get curious about our own strengths, beauty, peculiarities and frailties.

When we become fully present with our souls, we then become available to stand in witness of the souls of others. And, it is in this full presence, in this state of exposure, where soulful connections are made. With soulful connections comes the ability to coach and be coached.

Conclusion

As we noted way back in the preface, the art of being a Leader Coach requires a great deal of effort, discipline, and even sacrifice on the part of the leader. The beauty of this entire process is that in the course of serving others, the leader can also find peace and growth through the act of remaining in touch with his soul. Does this internal focus make the leader weak? Does it inhibit his ability to make tough decisions or to have the tough conversation? Most assuredly not. The ability to remain in touch with his own soul, as well as the ability to identify the needs of other's, strengthens what the Leader brings to the role.

Chapter 7

Presence

If you talk to any professional athlete, they will tell you that when they step between the lines on the baseball diamond, or the lines of the basketball court, it is all about having their head in the game. Michael Jordan, arguably the most talented player that the NBA has ever seen, will say that aside from natural talent and desire, that the difference between winning and losing is all about having your head in the game, or more aptly, "being in the zone." There is no doubting that Cleveland Cavalier and Utah Jazz fans know all about Michael's "being in the zone." Intense, focused, and hungry are all adjectives that describe the state of mind of a champion. They are the states of mind that all champions bring with them to whatever endeavor is at hand.

Like his athletic counterpart, when stepping into a coaching conversation, the Leader Coach must be fully present with his or her employee. The coaching conversation is not one that should be taken lightly or entered into on a rushed or hurried basis. Performance-based conversations, which may or may not lead to a formal performance improvement plan (PIP), can many times be "quick hits," and conducted with less preparation leading up to them. They may require a lesser time investment for the actual conversation, because the leader can often time rely upon subject matter expertise to direct an employee's future efforts. In these conversations, the leader many times *is* the expert in the given area, and, similarly to recalling a simple proven fact of mathematics can develop quick solutions for a problem an employee is having in delivering expected results.

However, the coaching conversation is *neither* directive nor directing in nature. As stated earlier, the coaching or developmental conversation is one that requires the leader to allay their "known" solutions, and employ the art of questioning, or the Socratic method of instruction as utilized in most law schools across the country; to *guide* the employee to find their own solutions. Because of both the intense nature, and potential impact, of this conversation, it requires the full presence of the leader.

In addition to full presence, it is imperative that the Leader Coach approaches the conversation *without* a fixed agenda, with a quiet mind, and free from other distractions that would inhibit the leader's full and undivided presence for the employee. For the absence of any of these conditions will diminish the value of the coaching conversation.

What does it mean to be *with* someone – an employee, a child, a friend, a spouse? For purposes of this discussion it means being fully present. Not just physically, but also mentally and emotionally. Remember, we shared with you that being an effective coach requires you to expose your soul in the process. There is a South African word *ubuntu*, which means "I am because we are." In other words, the coach's identity is also transformed by virtue of participating in the coaching conversation. Both parties become different people because of the interaction with one another.

Being *with* someone means that the mind is quiet, the environment conducive to open, honest communication, and that physical and emotional distractions have been addressed, prepared for, or set aside. Make no mistake, this presence is an investment that the employee can sense. Just as a spouse knows full well when we are not fully present for a conversation, the employee can sense when the coach is not fully engaged or present. What are the signs of not being present? Some would include, and certainly not be limited to: impatience, calendar distractions, interruptions from administrative assistants, telephone calls not being held, physical posture, defensiveness, or constantly reviewing a clock or an agenda. Any one of them is enough to undermine the process and to send an undesired signal to the employee that we are not with them.

How do we become present? We prepare for it. We can prepare by conducting self-examination, by receiving proper coaching ourselves, utilizing effective time management practices, as well as engaging in tactical preparation. This preparation could include scheduling considerations beyond time management, as well as creating the proper environment within your office, e.g. eliminating "piles" of paper, eliminating clutter, and making the office as welcoming and conducive to communication as possible.

Another method of tactical preparation may include scheduling a monthly breakfast or lunch session *out* of the office, where as a Leader Coach you will be completely free of the numerous distractions present in the office, and in an even more conducive mode for some serious career counseling with your player. The key is to keep this conversation purely focused on the employee, and *not* to fall into the trap of discussing ongoing projects or customer service issues. This is but one structure and practice that you can employ, and will be further discussed in Chapter 11. When we are fully present, we both *see* and *feel* the employee. We *see* their value, we *feel* their emotions, which may range from joy to fear, we sense their misunderstanding, and we can revel in their achievement. When we as leaders are fully present for our employees in this way, we are prepared to participate in rich, mutually rewarding, coaching conversations. It will also ultimately empower the group and allow you to elicit outstanding performance from the entire team, as all the individual relationships meld together to make the whole greater than the sum of its parts.

PREPARING FOR PRESENCE

Being present requires genuine intention. Leaders must prepare for presence. Yet, in a world of frantic activity, how does the Leader quiet himself for full presence? Again, it must be intentional. One coaching tool developed as a product of the speech acts, as discussed by John Searle, is the concept of Declaration, Intention, and Commitment.

By *declaration*, we mean that the player must make a declaration or utterance, similar to that of a public commitment, such as when sales people will commit to a quota or goal in the course of a sales meeting surrounded by their peers.

A player shows intent, or is *intentional*, when he or she determines the methodology by which the declaration will be made to come to life. This occurs when either structure or practices are employed that requires the player to live the declaration. With these structures or practices, goals are established, and sub-goals or milestones are created, and the player informs the coach of what role he or she may play in the attainment of these goals.

The *commitment* is in evidence when the intention is exhibited or some measure of proof is observable, i.e. a milestone is achieved, or the player takes an affirmative action that would denote engagement.

Likewise, when making the declaration that we are going to be a coach, there is a set of behaviors we must put in place in order to live our declaration. This set of behaviors shows intention to follow through on our declarations. Our commitment would be evident by our taking any of the above steps such as conducting self-examination, by receiving our own coaching, utilizing effective time management practices, as well as engaging in any of the tactical preparations which we discussed above, such as eliminating "piles" of paper, eliminating clutter, and making the office as welcoming and conducive to communication as possible.

The question the Leader Coach must ask himself is, "how am I showing intention to be fully present?" The answer is it takes work, and requires us to demonstrate our intent to be present. Through self-coaching or working with our own coaches, we as leaders can find the right set of behaviors for each of us to find our own presence. These sets of behaviors may include soul developing exercises such as:

- **Coaching:** seek out coaching from other coaches for ourselves.
- **Journaling:** capturing our own thoughts and feelings.
- **Exercise:** physical exertion is not only good for the body but also for the mind.
- **Family activities:** this includes "intentional downtime" where we re-charge our batteries, and serve the needs of our own family. Even things like household chores that permit us to become better connected such as the dishes, bath time for the kids, or helping homework, will produce great unexpected moments.

- **Activities that engage the spirit:** reading inspirational or "possibility" books that serve to create hope in our own souls.

Getting intentional for being present may also include tactical items such as:

- **Setting aside time:** on a calendar to think and to brainstorm by ourselves.
- **Ensuring the environment is free of distractions:** free of clutter, proper temperature, and that there is comfortable and appropriate seating.

BEING PRESENT

There are a number of things that the Leader Coach must do in order to prepare himself to being present for any of the conversations that he will be engaging in with the player. They include:

- **Listening:** is truly an art form. It requires both effort and focus.
- **Agenda:** set it aside! While as the coach you should have a broad outline of points that you want to cover, you also retain the ability of directing the flow of the conversation. A leader coach will be mindful to keep it as free flowing as possible, and to allow the player to determine the level of significance to attach to various aspects of the conversation.
- **Active observation:** we need to be watching our player for indicators from them that would include body language, eye contact, nervousness, and distraction.
- **Quiet Mind:** it is imperative that we can set aside our own issues and distractions, and to truly focus our energies on the player – his words, his actions, his emotions.
- **Curious:** we demonstrate our presence by allowing our curiosity to run wild, and to interact with the player by asking questions that provoke more commentary from him. Remember, this is their time to express themselves, and

through our questions, to discover answers and pathways to be followed.
- **Judgment free:** this is not the time for assessments, but rather time for us to be listening, evaluating, and synthesizing our own thoughts.
- **Be Still:** as the coach it is important that we are truly "locked in" on our player, and not distracted by potential disruptions from assistants, the telephone, blackberry, or other outside sources.

Another great resource available for the coach to utilize in the furtherance of the 'Being Present' skills are the wonderful books previously mentioned authored by Stephen C. Lundin, Harry Paul, and John Christensen that comprise the fun but extremely valuable *Fish!* series of books.

TACTICS TO BE PRESENT

Planning

In Today's hustle and bustle corporate environment, leaders spend significant time preparing for strategy planning sessions, project meetings, and developing presentations for their bosses and other stakeholders. This being said, why do so many take little to no time to prepare for meetings with their subordinates? Therein lays the difference between a Leader/Manager and a Leader Coach. The Leader Coach is intentional, and does approach these meetings with his or her *players* with the same level of intensity, and places perhaps an even higher significance on these meetings because he does care.

The Leader Coach has both the awareness and the diligence to prepare for these critical engagements with as much effort as those meetings that focus on serving himself because as a servant leader, he knows how important these meetings are to not only the individual, but exponentially, to the organization as well. As a result, it is not uncommon for the Coach to spend more time in preparation than the player.

Environment

As previously noted while discussing the tactical preparation that the coach needs to engage in, establishing an environment that is both quiet and conducive to actively listening to the player without distraction is critical. For this reason, a quiet restaurant with a certain degree of privacy and intimacy is ideal to the coaching process. If in fact you opt to remain in the office, it will require additional effort to safeguard against interruption and in creating the environment.

Time Management

As we previously noted, each session must be afforded the necessary time requisite for the coach and player to interact appropriately. An average length of time for these sessions would be 60 to 90 minutes. While not completely open ended, unless exigent circumstances exist, these sessions should not last longer than two hours, as exceeding this limit usually brings about a diminishing return.

Recognizing and Admitting When Sessions should be re-scheduled

As the Leader Coach, it is completely your responsibility to have the courage to admit when you are not totally present, and to either make alternative arrangements or to reschedule the session. Conversely, in chapter 9, we will discuss the value of the Social Conversation. If through the social conversation, we find the player distracted, we should reschedule as well.

CONCLUSION

The true Leader Coach serves his player by being present whenever communicating with the player, but especially during sessions dedicated to coaching. Painful as it is, both authors must confess that they have each heard from their respective spouses something along the lines of, "I wish you put one-half the effort into our marriage, or listening to me, as you do into the people who work for you." Ouch. We share this because we hope it serves to illustrate that nobody is perfect, and that we all have to be *aware* of the importance of being present for all of those whom we consider to be important in our lives.

Chapter 8

Risk

If you thought being a Leader Coach was an easy task, free from peril and risk, simply because you are approaching the relationship from the vantage point of boss, or superior, well, surprise, this is not the case at all. Whether that player you are coaching is a valued employee, a friend, or even your own child, there is an inherent element of risk always present. If you are truly a coach, then *you* have an emotional investment in the relationship! Inherent to any relationship is risk. This risk may even come in the form of job security if you find yourself in the position of coaching a peer or a superior who is not receptive to the coaching, or more likely, it is simply your own heart and soul that will be at risk. We've heard that as leaders we leave our fingerprints on those whom we lead – it can either be in a positive or negative manner – we can either lift up, or push down these people, all the while living vicariously through our players and their achievements.

Upon completing their courses of study, doctors are administered the Hippocratic Oath, in which they vow to do no harm. Sometimes we wonder if maybe a coach should not take a similar oath. As coaches we have an incredible opportunity to do good, or conversely, to do bad, hence the reference to fingerprints. As we said in the Preface, coaching is not for the faint of heart. It is both the most rewarding, and challenging, thing that we can do as leaders. Inherent with this opportunity is risk. Risk to the player, as well as to ourselves, especially when we must conduct a coaching session that is performance or behavior oriented, since the player will undoubtedly approach such a meeting from a defensive posture.

So what is the risk to you as coach? First and foremost, this risk comes in the form of the danger that your relationship may face if your coaching is either misconstrued or ill-received even under the best of circumstances. For even under these best of circumstances, when all of the 'rules' are followed, and the player *knows* that the coach loves him, and has his very best interests at heart, there is grave risk that the coaching may be rejected, and the relationship can be damaged. This risk exists all the more any time a coach engages in an active supportive intervention, with the expectation that the coaching will prompt a declaration of ownership by the player, followed by a subsequent shift in behavior on the part of the player. The good news is that when the relationship is based on trust, and the lines of communication stay open, this damage can be temporary, or minimized, and the relationship can ultimately be strengthened as a result.

Most typically, the use of the terms 'coach' and 'player' makes the average person think of the athletic arena. To this end, the relationship between coach and player as illustrated in the world of professional sports where a *professional* coach is tasked with *extracting* the very best from a *professional* athlete is but one example, but remains analogous enough to bear examination. This is perhaps the most difficult form of coaching because of the inherent attitudes and egos that often accompany an athlete's multi-million dollar contract. Let's face it, when someone is being paid millions of dollars, it is pretty easy for that person to believe that they are beyond the need of coaching. By the same token, the truly gifted athlete welcomes this coaching, because he wants to maximize his potential and talents, and views his relationship with his coach as a collaborative effort.

One of the best modern day professional athletic coaches, and truly an expert at this craft of collaboration is Phil Jackson. The Zen Master of the NBA's coaching ranks, Phil regularly purchases books for his players to read while traveling from city to city. He picks these books based on either the players' interests, or on a specific need he perceives in the player's professional or personal life. He cares, and is willing to risk this relationship, by taking this positive step.

Some more about Phil's credentials as a basketball head coach. As a player, he was a member of the world champion New York Knicks. As the Head Coach of the Chicago Bulls and Los Angeles Lakers, he has on three separate occasions, won back-to-back-to-back championships, for a total of nine world championships. He and Red Auerbach of the Boston Celtics *are* in fact the coaches with the most championships bar none. Most assuredly, he has done this by employing some rather unorthodox practices, and doing things his way. He has done so by being analytical, insightful, and by challenging his players from a unique spiritual and inspirational perspective. From the day he became a head coach in the National Basketball Association, Jackson inspired a shared vision of winning the world championship, but not doing so in the same win-at-any-cost attitude of New York Yankee owner George Steinbrenner of Major League Baseball, but rather from a more Zen-like perspective. In this respect, Jackson was more interested in winning by having his assistant coaches and players focus on *being present*, and to be thinking in terms of *team*, and their common goal, rather than individual achievement.

Lots of outsiders, ignorant of the challenges associated with that of coaching and inspiring true superstars, have said that Jackson had an easy time as a coach because he had the likes of Michael Jordan, Scottie Pippen, Dennis Rodman, and a cast of winning players to win six championships with the Chicago Bulls, and then Shaquille O'Neal and Kobe Bryant in Los Angeles for the other three rings. Nothing could be further from the truth. The six New York Yankees teams of 2001-2006 have cost the ownership in excess of $1.2 billion without a single championship ring to show for this sizeable investment! The most recent playoff debacle in 2006 is further proof that a $200 million payroll of individual superstars certainly lends credence to the argument that money and talented *individuals* are not the stuff of championships. *Performance*, coupled with actively sharing an inspired vision, and the ability to sublimate, and then replace the "me" with "we," is the stuff of winners. The key remains with having the willingness to risk the individual one on one relationship, and in Jackson's case, potentially his entire coaching career, with this unique approach to coaching.

COMMUNICATION

Okay so now you know that at least one of us is a big Phil Jackson fan. To avoid even the appearance of impropriety, and before we alienate any of the millions of Yankees fans out there who are hopefully coughing up the money for this book, we acknowledge that sometimes, the coach can only be held so accountable for the actions, or failures of his players. Certainly Dusty Baker, the now former skipper of the Chicago Cubs will agree with that statement.

To the truly avid baseball fan, Joe Torre, the often embattled manager of the New York Yankees is nothing short of brilliant. He is also a class act. He was a class act while playing third base for the St. Louis Cardinals, and now lends dignity and grace to the management ranks. As the Yankees skipper he has taken them to the playoffs eleven straight seasons, won the division title nine straight times, and actually won the World Series four out of the first five years that he was at the helm. The frustration in New York, and particularly in the owner's box, is that for the next six seasons, there has been a World Series defeat, two league championship losses, and three abrupt first round exits. To the less than informed fan, who may only witness Joe from the screen in a bar, or while waiting for a table for dinner, he appears to be cool, emotionless, and extremely reserved while watching a tight game from the dugout. Whether the Yankees are winning or being clobbered, his emotions remain in check. What these latter fans don't know is that Joe is actually a rather brilliant communicator, and views open, honest communication as one of the keys to managing a team of twenty five very diverse players. His post-game interviews certainly reveal that this is an articulate man with much to say!

What is the key to Joe's unprecedented success? He in fact has identified communicating as having five distinct requirements.

- **Identify individual needs:** A good coach determines what each individual needs in the way of communication, albeit help with his physical skills, e.g. a batter's swing, a pitcher's delivery; emotional support, e.g. motivation, or a swift kick in the pants, or whack to the side of the head; or simply someone to lend a sympathetic ear.

- **Time Your Talks:** Timing is everything. If someone is not going to be receptive to what you have to say, don't bother saying it. The key is to know when the time is right. Joe seems to have taken this skill to an art form. What will probably become a classic example is the manner in which he counseled with baseball's highest paid player in the summer of 2006 as he languished in a three month slump. Alex Rodriguez – "A-Rod" to his fans and detractors alike – needed coaching so badly, that he did not even recognize it. This need for coaching, and the manner in which Joe Torre conducted it was actually a cover feature story for Sports Illustrated. Weeks went by before Torre called A-Rod into the visiting managers office in Seattle's Safeco Field, and began his intervention. In subsequent interviews, Rodriguez acknowledges that there was no doubt that Joe Torre sincerely cared about him individually, as well as the good of the team. It's all in the timing.
- **Acknowledge emotions:** At times the Leader Coach is a father confessor. Players, especially athletes, will bring a range of emotions to the table running the gamut from fear, superstition (hey, I'll admit to wearing the same warm ups all season without washing them), and irrational anxiety, to over confidence and arrogance. A good coach knows how to acknowledge and either deflect or deflate these emotions. Joe Torre knows.
- **Get issues on the table:** Open communication requires that issues get put out there for discussion. To not do so means that these problems will only fester and get worse and larger in scope. Just as bad news does not get better with age, problems that are ignored only grow into bigger problems.
- **Use team meetings to clear the air and increase motivation for the group as a whole:** Closed door clubhouse meetings are not uncommon during a 162 game baseball season. During a 2006 swoon by his Chicago White Sox, Manager Ozzie Guillen held one such meeting, and the results were evident in the manner in which hitters came out hitting, pitchers came out pitching, and winning became a team goal again.

So where does this fit in with risk? In Joe's case, he merely has to pick up a copy of any of the New York tabloids and he knows *instantly* whether he is being successful in his endeavors as a Leader Coach. If the box score of his teams' collective and individual performances does not indicate success, or provide him with enough feedback, he can read the New York City columnists who are always quick to write a commentary on what they observe. Or, if he is really a glutton for punishment, he can walk down the hall to owner George Steinbrenner's office, and hear from "the Boss" exactly how effective or ineffective his methods have been, almost as quickly as he utilizes them. If all else fails, he can simply wait to hear about them in sound bites on ESPN. Feedback is important for providing the coach with additional insights and direction. The risk comes in the form of having to choose and implement a course of action. On a team such as the Yankees this could involve multiple, simultaneous choices which in itself presents a challenge to the Leader Coach.

CARING

The most important thing a leader, and coach, can show to his player, is pure, honest caring. Everyone, and we mean everyone, wants to feel cared about, accepted, and seeks unconditional love everywhere they live, work, and breathe. Whether it is from Grandma Mary, or Mrs. Ward the 4th grade teacher, or Coach Miller out on the ball field, we seek acceptance and approval, but most of all, someone who *cares* about old #1.

Lou Holtz, another coach of notable reputation, believes that the one question that every player wants to hear a resounding "yes!" to is "do you care about me?"

So how is a coach, like any of us, caught up in the propriety of the workplace, supposed to show that he cares? We begin by creating the proper environment. An environment that is free of criticism and criticality, and full of compassion, and genuine concern. A leader who can, and does, ask about the personal life of his player, because he knows enough to do so, will quickly earn the respect of the player. Knowing about the player's outside interests will also contribute to building an environment of loyalty and respect.

Author James C. Hunter, in his book *The Servant* says that it is important that the coach must *love* their players, meaning that he can place the player's interests ahead of his own, and to truly be there. In this sense, he utilizes the word *love* as a verb, and means that actions, more than words, communicates this feeling. It means opening his own heart and exposing his own soul by sharing experiences and demonstrating necessary compassion. The greater risks here are the potential for outright rejection and hurt feelings, or the fact that the Coach may be more committed than the player.

TOUGH LOVE

What happens when we compromise a quantitative standard in an effort to help a player? Sam does not hit the monthly minimum required by his sales contract, or Johnny does not maintain the grade point average requisite to participating in athletics. Should we lower the scale? Do we ignore the standards? If we do, what message does this send to the other players who ARE achieving and/or maintaining the standards? Do we actually help them, or does this leniency merely put us on the precipice of a slippery slope? As with our own children, coaches must be prepared to risk the relationship by adhering to standards and to force the environment to be more conducive to helping the player achieve the stated standards.

It is critical to remember that there is great truth to the old adage "they won't care what you know, until they know how much you care." Christ could teach his disciples principles of the Gospel only *after* they knew how much he truly loved them. Likewise, an errant teenager will not be receptive to corrective actions or constructive criticism unless we first approach them in a spirit of love. Players at the office are no different. If they truly believe that we care about them first, and want to improve their performance secondarily, the coach will most assuredly be successful in modifying less than desired behavior, and help the player to in fact achieve the established standards.

The roles that Leader Coaches have to fill are truly multi-faceted. Leader Coaches sometimes are called upon to simply hold the line. It may require making and then enforcing an unpopular decision on an individual or on the group as a whole. The key question that the coach must ask is whether this decision will promote growth and positive change in the player(s) or whether it is merely to make a point or to flaunt his authority. If it is the former, then it is a positive and should be carried out. If it is the latter, then the Leader Coach has stepped over the line and abused his authority, which may have an adverse impact on his relationship with the player(s).

Years ago, while stationed with the United States Army in the Federal Republic of Germany, the cavalry squadron that one of the authors was assigned to, had two mottos that characterized the manner in which it operated, and valued its personnel. The mission statement was "Care the Most, Operate the Best, and Cover ourselves in Glory." The companion statement of "Mission First, People Always," seemed to succinctly state that while mission accomplishment was of paramount importance, we would only do so by recognizing and treating our soldiers as our most valued resource. With people who feel cared about, are inspired, and are thus willing to do whatever is necessary, mission accomplishment, even in the face of overwhelming odds, is a virtual certainty. Take any of those elements out of the equation, and all of a sudden, valuable and much needed materiel is not delivered in a timely manner, maintenance goes unperformed, training ceases to be effective, and the war machine grinds to a halt. Even in an autocratic environment such as the military, if a Leader Coach is willing to apply these simple standards of effective leadership, great results can be accomplished.

The risk for the Leader who does not sincerely care for his player and communicate this concern to them, is that they may not fully engage; the battle or sales campaign may be lost; and the organization ultimately suffers the loss of talent these players bring to the table. It is imperative that the Leader Coach be willing to risk his own standing when putting the needs of his team first. If the players perceive anything different, the Leader Coach becomes ineffective and will have to be replaced.

More Tips on Caring

Colin Powell has worn many hats in his career of public service. This service has ranged from commanding millions of soldiers, sailors, and airmen in uniform as Chairman of the Joint Chiefs of Staff, to advising Presidents of the United States as National Security Advisor, and later, as Secretary of State. Having heard him speak on several occasions, the man exudes both confidence and grace. His secret you ask? He speaks and personifies the qualities of selflessness, sacrifice, and caring.

During visits to the troops in Saudi Arabia during the Persian Gulf War, Powell made quite a contrast to his commander on the ground, General Norman Schwarzkopf. Powell, reserved, a listener, and well aware of the power of his words, in contrast to "Stormin' Norman" who was quick to explode and to let a subordinate know exactly where to go and how to get there. Powell believed that players would value the words of the coach more if they believed that the coach was enduring the same hardships as they were. What it really meant is that if the troops were suffering in 120 degree heat, as a leader, you were hot too. The difference is that you did not sweat. Troops, players, subordinates, need to know that they are cared about, and that they can count on you as the Leader Coach to model the way in both character and action.

Conclusion

The true Leader Coach is willing to risk his relationship, his standing, even his very status, with the player when he enters into a supportive intervention or session of performance management. He begins by reassuring the player that he does care; that he cares enough about the player individually to risk the unpleasantness that may ensue as the result of being the messenger with a particular message.

It means caring enough about the individual because of the relationship that is already in place, and wanting to make it even better by taking any and all steps necessary to help the player improve.

It all begins by loving the player, and being truly committed to the player's own growth, and out of a desire to leave positive fingerprints on the back of the player.

Part IV

*Practice:
The Art of Conversation*

We are now ready to move beyond a discussion of the Leader Coach as an individual and the relationship between the coach and player, and to delve into the actual art of being a coach. In these three chapters, entitled Involved, Resolved, and Evolved, we will examine the actual practice of conducting the Social, Performance, and Developmental coaching conversations.

In the chapter entitled Involved, we will begin the Social Conversation where we first become involved in the life of the player, and must demonstrate genuine interest in the lives of those whom we lead and coach. Personal knowledge of family, outside interests, hobbies, and ancillary challenges with immediate and extended family is key.

In Resolved, we begin the Performance-oriented Conversation. The coach must resist the temptation to simply mentor or share how he did it. Use of the Socratic Method is of paramount importance. In this conversation we aid the player in resolving performance issues. A Leader Coach should have more questions than answers for his or her players, and use these questions as the means by which growth and development takes place in the player.

Finally, in Evolved, we conduct the Developmental Conversation. This is where the skills of Supportive Intervention come into play, and the player assumes ownership for his or her behavior and future endeavors. It is imperative that both the coach and the player be willing to expose their hearts and their souls by showing mutual concern and involvement. It is by far the most difficult, yet most rewarding, of the three discussions. In essence, through a series of developmental conversations, the player's skills evolve to the next level by establishing a framework in which the player will be coached and simultaneously implement these new strategies because *action* is the critical key to real development.

Will you be an expert after reading these three chapters as well as those that precede and follow them? Probably not, but you will have a greater appreciation of the role, and will hopefully have garnered some insights that will make you better prepared to handle the challenges that will come your way.

Remember, the best way to be a coach is to be coachable yourself, and to always strive for the next growth lesson.

Chapter 9

Involved

There are only two major life forces that we all encounter each and every day, and how we allow these forces to impact our personality, our actions, and our inner person remains a choice within our control. These two forces are *love* and *fear*. We have discussed both of them at length, but as we approach the art of communicating with our players, nothing is more important than recognizing and dealing with these two incredibly divergent emotions.

With love, we find every positive emotion that life has to offer. We are filled with happiness, joy, hope, excitement, anticipation, and even the *spirit* of Christmas when the end of the year rolls around.

Unfortunately, fear brings every negative emotion to our door. We must contend with sadness, frustration, jealousy, failure, dread, a lack of hope, and even depression.

Fortunately, we all have our own agency, and the ability to *choose* which force of nature we will allow into our lives. Recall if you will, Charles Dickens' *A Christmas Carol,* and the metamorphosis experienced by Ebenezer Scrooge, and the joy and glee with which he greets Christmas morning and prompts the young lad in the street to procure the largest goose from the butcher and to deliver it to the Cratchet residence. We all find hope and are uplifted by the change experienced by this former curmudgeon, and can feel his joy, even if only vicariously.

Perhaps an even greater, albeit fictional, example of the impact that the leader coach can have on the people around him is found in Frank Capra's Christmas tale, *It's A Wonderful Life*. Here again, one man, George Bailey, touches countless lives of those around him either for good, or in his absence, for bad. This is the role of the true Leader Coach; to positively impact the lives of those around him.

As you may have gathered from the introduction to this section, aptly entitled Practice: The Art of Conversation, in chapters 9, 10 and 11 we are going to get to the very heart of this book, and what we consider to be the very crux of being a Leader Coach: communication. These are the Leader Coach skills for which we've prepared our souls; these are the how-to steps to transform one's approach from Manager to Leader to Leader Coach, and the very means by which we impact the lives of those around us.

If a 9-year old child observed his mother at work in the typical Fortune 300 company office, what would he describe his mother's work to be? Most likely it would be meeting with different people during the day and talking. This talking would be either in person or on the telephone; conference calls or computer-generated same time presentations, but in all of these situations, she would be practicing the art of talking. The single greatest tool of any Manager, Leader, or Leader Coach is in fact the art of conversation. This conversation can be directive, understanding, appreciative, compelling, mean spirited, questioning, or influential. But regardless of approach, style, or intention, it is conversation that must be the primary tool of today's Managers, Leaders, and Leader Coaches. While e-mail, or more precisely, instant messaging, can be considered a form of conversation, it is much too frequently, and incorrectly, used by Managers (note Leaders are not mentioned) to communicate with peers and players about topics that would be much better suited for a verbal or face-to-face meeting. The idea of conversation as the primary tool of Leaders and Leader Coaches was something that Terry picked up at Georgetown University's Leadership Coaching program, especially supported by Kim Krisco's book, *Leadership and the Art of Conversation*. Further, in Terry's work with Dr. Neil Stroul, when he was being coached by Neil as an executive, Neil frequently discussed the three conversations Leaders must master: Social, Performance, and Developmental. The chapters that follow are largely based upon the theories picked up from these references, other resources on leadership coaching, and supported by years of hands on experience.

Couple these techniques with the previously discussed practices of supportive intervention as mentioned in the chapters on Risk, Courage, and Congruence, and we quickly discern that masterful communication is a critical skill that a Leader and Leader Coach must develop, utilize, and constantly strive to improve.

We don't presuppose that these are the only ways to transform one's style from Leader to Leader Coach, they are but a few of the approaches that we have found practical, and grounded in our 50 years of collective experience in both the corporate and military environments.

Involved – The Social Conversation

In far too many organizations today, those individuals who are fortunate enough to fill the more senior level positions are treated like, and unfortunately behave, as if they are royalty or heads of state. Their schedules are micromanaged to the minute, interactions with those they lead are orchestrated, information they receive from those they lead is often times sanitized, bulletized, edited, disinfected, as well as compartmentalized. The unfortunate result of these processes and structures, are that they prevent the executive from hearing what is really going on both personally and professionally in the lives of those they lead. Granted, the rewards and incentives that senior executives receive should be in direct correlation to the challenges that they face, as well as recognition of the personal sacrifices that they make in leading large organizations. Conversely, based on the compensation received by these executives, organizations understandably want and expect incredible productivity and effectiveness for the investment being made. But, all too often the structures that are put in place to wisely manage an executive's time also prevents them from ever really knowing those they lead. Furthermore, for those not inclined to take an interest in their players' lives, these structures help to reinforce an alienation of the Leader from the players.

We're not naïve enough to believe that leaders should know every person whom they lead, nor have the time to recall individual situations in each of their lives. However, when the great leaders of the past spoke, somehow they spoke directly to us – they were keenly aware of the environment and emotions of a situation. And it is this type of personal connection that leaders must make to step into leadership and coaching.

If you recall from Chapter 2, we gave the example of the Manager that burns a path between his office and the bathroom without ever acknowledging those that he passes. This manager is either so task-focused to the point that it is detrimental, or chooses to believe that he does not have time for idle chat which in itself is a shortcoming, for it is in these quick and quiet minutes that a great deal of good can be accomplished. That being said, there are some who would argue that this is a waste of the manager's time, and if there is something to be completed, then it is incumbent upon that manager to get it done as quickly and expertly as possible. Step back, and ask yourself: would *you* want to work for someone who views this as normal behavior? In all likelihood, if we met this manager outside of work, we'd think he's a nice guy – wound a little tight, but a nice guy. It's just that inside the walls of the office building he's too busy to notice those around him.

How might a leader approach their "bio-break" in a different way? The leader would walk down the hallway, head up, wanting to greet and meet people along the way. The leader would make the effort to learn as many people's name as possible, and call as many by their name as possible. The leader would stop and have a brief conversation with those he met, remembering their personal situations from the last time they spoke. The leader would share (if appropriate) what he is working on and ask for input or ideas from every level of player in the organization.

Why would the leader take these additional steps to complete a simple jaunt to the bathroom? Because he cares, because he values others, because he respects them as people, because he's interested in their lives and opinions – because great leaders love! Great leaders show their love by showing an interest in those they lead. Great leaders are visible, accessible, and approachable. Back to the idea of royalty, how many managers have each of us known whom we would never think of knocking on their office door? We would never knock on that door because we think: that's a scary place; he's too busy to talk with me; he's not interested in my opinion, he doesn't really care what we have to say, or he doesn't know me. In essence we as managers build this destructive or growth inhibiting facade of 'royalty' by our behaviors. We might say, "my door is always open", yet our actions say, "I dare you to knock on my door."

When a Leader invests the time for social conversations with those he leads, he is taking the first step in "compelling others to want to follow." When a Leader invests the time for social conversation it puts meaning into the phrase, "I have an open door policy."

Get Curious

How does one make this shift from the ranks of "Royalty" (Manager) to that of Leader using conversation, especially if it's not something that comes instinctively? It begins in the same manner as we identified in Chapters 1 and 2, in that it requires a conscious shifting of one's focus of attention from ourselves to others around us. To become a Master of the Social Conversation, we must first have a genuine interest in those we lead. We must fully see the worth of every person and acknowledge that worth by sharing our time and interest. You might be saying, "That is easy for an extrovert, but I'm an introverted person and not a real strong conversationalist." To that we say, "hogwash," whatever that really means.

Terry is by nature an introverted person, and yes, walking into a party with a room full of people he doesn't know, still gives him the heebee-geebees; but what we are talking about here is much different. In fact, if you are an introvert we would say that you should approach the players on the floor the same way you approach a room full of strangers. Approach one person at a time, see the unique value in that person, and get curious. "Curious" is a beautiful, powerful word for a leader. Think back to a time when there was a person, a thing, a situation, or body of knowledge about which you would have done just about anything to find out more about. Think about the emotions you felt, the surge of energy, and the joy that you experienced when you merely thought about the object of your curiosity. Recall the effort you put into researching, questioning, and processing information shared about the topic. This desire to understand is what we call "getting curious."

Now, if we apply this emotion to the typical Monday morning social conversation in the office, it might go something like this.

> "Jim, good morning, how was your weekend?" asks Sarah.
> "My weekend was okay, thanks for asking Sarah," says Jim.
> "Jim about the reports I asked you to review last Friday, did you get a chance to give them a glance?" Sarah questions.
> "No. I really did not have the time, but I'll take care of it this morning," Jim answers.

On the surface, this sounds like a pleasant enough greeting between Sarah and her employee, Jim, as they get back to work on Monday. But, now, let's throw in a little curiosity to spice up the conversation.

> "Jim, good morning, how was your weekend?" asks Sarah.
> "My weekend was okay, thanks for asking Sarah," says Jim.
> "What made your weekend okay? Did you and the family do something enjoyable," asks Sarah with a smile.
> "Actually, our weekend wasn't all that enjoyable, we ran from activity to activity with the kids, and somehow in between activities we ran over to my mother's house to make sure she was okay," Jim answers.
> "I know *exactly* what you are talking about Jim. It's like a blur sometimes, isn't it? I know how full family life can be," Sarah offers.
> "It just seems to get crazier and crazier," agrees Jim.
> "By the way, how is your mother? You mentioned she was having some surgery last week," said Sarah.
> "Thanks for remembering. The surgery went according to plan, but she'll have a couple of tough weeks during the recovery."
> "If you feel the need to check on her during the week, let's talk about a way I can help you out by covering for you or moving things around here a bit. And Jim, if there is anything you'd like to talk about, I'm willing to listen," suggests Sarah.
> "Sarah, that's a nice offer, I appreciate the support," says Jim.

At this point in the conversation, Sarah has awareness that it might not be the appropriate time to ask about the reports she asked Jim to review just last Friday. She can follow up on this later by dropping by his office. By following up later, it will give her yet another chance to check-in with Jim again.

How does Jim feel after these two conversations? The first conversation seems like a normal, cordial conversation between manager and subordinate, and it's not out of the ordinary for Sarah to have pleasantly acknowledged Jim and followed up with a work related question. But, how does Jim feel? Most likely, he's saying in his own mind, "oh great, I had a lousy weekend, and now Sarah's asking me about reports that she just requested on Friday." Seemingly, a pretty typical reaction on his part.

In the second conversation, Sarah got curious. Her follow up question of "what made your weekend okay" was more open-ended. If the Leader approaches these conversations in this way, with open ended questions that have sincerity about wanting to know someone, the Leader will be surprised about what he learns. The learning could be about the player's personal situation, about a hobby you never considered, or a skill that the player only exhibits when they are away from the office, but could very well be applied at work – that's the beauty of getting curious.

Another decided set of 'plusses' to the second conversation is that by getting curious, Sarah learned about some personal issues that may be affecting Jim. She was then able to better gauge his emotions and feelings, as well as his potential ability to focus on work. Jim in turn learned that Sarah really does care about him, as evidenced by the concern she expressed by remembering his mother's surgery, showing empathy toward his situation, as well as the manner in which she offered to help. Sarah's curiosity stemmed from a genuine interest in Jim, and as a result Jim probably has a stronger desire to support Sarah and what she is attempting to accomplish on behalf of the organization. Which Sarah would you be more compelled to want to follow?

While the answer to the question may appear obvious, we are also certain that some of you are still wondering if this stuff really works. Will the effort to become a more social leader *really* make a difference? Will simply becoming more social around the office really add to my credibility as a leader, and allow me to have a larger impact with my players? The short answer to both questions is yes.

Don's experience of going into a room full of people with whom he is not acquainted is different than Terry's. While neither a nervous introvert nor gregarious extrovert, Don found himself faced with the decision of just what kind of person he wanted to be for the rest of his life. Through his position at church, serving in a lay ministry, and visiting seven different congregations on a regular rotating basis, he is always thrust into this position. While it took a great deal of time and practice, as well as a conscious desire to be genuine, Don is now able to walk into these different congregations and interact with a great deal of effectiveness. The key is that he genuinely cares about these people, and desires to *serve* them. Did it happen overnight? Most assuredly not, but with a desire to be genuine and to fill the needs of these people, it quickly became habit and then second nature.

The beauty of being human is that we can change. The desire to be genuinely interested in, and to serve, the people around us can quickly become a habit. This habit becomes who you are, and who other people want to emulate. It is the very means by which you, the Coach, continue your own journey of enlightenment, becoming a better, happier, more fulfilled you. Imagine the self-actualization that you will experience as a Leader Coach when someone who works for you, or more importantly, when your own child says, "I want to be just like you." Can there be any greater compliment or validation?

The beauty of this experience is that it carries over to the other aspects of our life. What may start in our "Sunday" life may extend into our business persona. Imagine how an agent in Boston or New Jersey feels when the Divisional Vice President arrives from Richmond, and can readily ask a personal question about a family member, a hobby, or major event in the person's life. It is the most powerful bonding, and ultimate teaching tool available to the Leader Coach. However, it must have as its primary ingredient genuine concern, and a desire to serve. It is most decidedly evolutionary, having been built on the one on one conversation that has taken place previously.

Another great, if not fictional example of how this change can occur, is evidenced by the character played by Bill Murray in the movie *Groundhog Day*. While enduring the challenge of living precisely the same day over and over again as he awoke each morning, Phil Connors (Murray) transforms himself from a self-absorbed prima donna frustrated by this strange twist of fate, into a man of multi talents, intent on serving the community by saving children falling out of trees, changing flat tires for elderly women, performing the Heimlich maneuver on a choking man, and quickly becoming the source of sage advice sought out by young and old alike. From learning the art of ice sculpting and mastering the piano, to learning a foreign language and memorizing classical poetry, Phil became a *social* being. The key to his success: his desire to interact with the people around him, and the conscious shift of his focus from himself to others. P.S. The good news is that he ends up with the girl at the end of the movie too!

A Purpose to Serve

In Chapter 2, we spoke of those characteristics that separate the Manager from the Leader and how we believe it comes from the focus of attention moving from self to others. Just a quick word on purpose, for the past decade there has been a great deal written on "purpose", and how each of us can find and live more fulfilled lives by living our purpose. Case in point, in *The Purpose Driven Life* by Rick Warren, a New York Times best seller for umpteen weeks, Warren puts the spotlight on each person finding their purpose. We certainly think it a noble and worthy cause to search within oneself to find one's purpose; but, one thing is clear, if you're in the role of leader, your purpose, at least in part, needs to be to serve others – to include those whom you lead. It is this mindset of serving others that will lead to a curiosity and appreciation of our players and their worth. And it is this appreciation and worth that will move us into rich social conversations with them. With these rich social conversations those that you lead will know that you've taken a keen interest in them.

Tactics

So you're now convinced that to show love and respect for their players, the Leader and Leader Coach should master the social conversation. If you've been someone socially awkward in the past, how will this come to pass? First, you must declare your desire to become more socially aware, as well as your desire to master this skill. Working with a coach will certainly make this easier to accomplish. Second, by actively practicing the art of conversing you will begin to develop new habits around having social conversations with your players.

A quick side note on practice. We'll speak much more about practice in Chapter 11, but for now a quick primer. We believe that development (growing one's skill or ability) simply requires a change of habit. In the development or improvement of a skill, we are asked to exhibit a new or improved set of behaviors to enhance our desired result. In the instance of Social Conversation, we would say that the Manager who has not mastered social conversation would need to develop a new set of behaviors to get the desired result of having rich social conversations with those that work for the Manager. We'll also see in Chapter 11, it is very likely that the Manager will also need to develop a new mind set and feelings about the value of social conversation before being able to exhibit these new behaviors. For now though, let's assume that the Manager is fully committed to developing a new mastery of social conversation with his team. With a strong commitment to develop this new skill, what does the Manager need to do? The answer is simple: practice. Just like any new skill, to master a behavior one needs to practice. Be it a new golf swing, a new song on a guitar, or getting started in writing, one needs practice; and, it is through consistent practice that one develops the new skill. By the way, this is where the power of coaching comes in, as it is through the coaching conversation where the player identifies new skills to be developed, and establishes new practices to help hone these skills. Yet again we digress to chapter 11, for now let us share some ideas with you on ways you might practice your new found commitment to social conversation with your players. Some of the practices that have worked for us include:

- **Office location:** pick out an office that requires you to more regularly socialize with your players. We can recall countless times when our peers and managers have intentionally positioned their offices so they would have less socialization with their players. Early in Terry's career he worked with an executive that demanded a bathroom be put in his office, because he did not want to use the same bathroom as his players. Our advice to you: don't jump at the chance to move away from your team – move closer to them.

- **Meeting agenda management:** Start every meeting with a check-in. What in the heck is a check-in? Well it's just a quick way for a team when it first starts its meeting to "check-in" with each other. How are we feeling? Want to see a bunch of executives squirm, ask them to check-in at the start of a meeting. As awkward as it may feel at first, your team will get it eventually. With practice it will become easy and productive. By the way, the idea of the check-in is simply a quick method for each of us to share what's happened in our lives recently and to share how we're feeling. Once folks get comfortable with "checking in" it's amazing what can be learned about one another and how we can develop an understanding why one of our team members or players is disengaged as a result of something really disrupting his/her life. And, it's amazing how much closer the Leader's team will become once they've put it to practice.
- **Calendar management:** Ever notice in your work life (and your personal life for that matter) how frequently you run from activity to activity without a minute in between, some days being so hectic that there's no time to eat. In this state of frenetic activity, we have less chance for social conversation. If one doesn't have time to stop for a sandwich, how are you ever going to justify slowing down to have "non-productive" conversation with someone? All managers and leaders need to become more disciplined owners of their calendars. One sure practice to provide for the possibility of having more, rich social conversations is keeping time for pause (recovery) in one's calendar. This practice of pause and recovery was raised by Jim Loehr and Tony Schwartz in their work **The Power of Full Engagement:** *Managing Energy, Not Time, is the key to high performance and personal renewal.* The theory behind their coaching practice of high performing athletes, which they have extended into corporate coaching, is that great athletes are called upon to exhibit peak performance

for relatively short periods, followed by periods of recovery. And, it is this practice of recovery that prepares them for the next performance. Simply view a tennis player between points, or a baseball hitter (or pitcher) between pitches, or a defensive lineman between snaps; all have mastered the ability to pause and recover between times when they're expected to perform at peak levels. A manager that fails to pause and recover is also a manager whose performance will invariably diminish over time. And there's one way to be sure one will skip practice of any kind: when one is in the state of exhaustion. The point: take command of your calendar and ensure that there is time for pause and time available for social conversation as you pass from one engagement (or meeting) to another. Another Calendar Management practice is scheduling time for socialization. Terry has managed a number of site closures. When a team is enduring this type of incredible change, the need for social contact between coach and players is greatly heightened. In this situation, even when filling the role of the Grim Reaper, the Leader Coach needs to book one hour every morning and afternoon to simply "walk the site," without a preformatted agenda.

The purpose is strictly to touch base with those being led, and to gain an understanding and appreciation of what is going on with your players, with your customers, and with the change *all* are living through. The last note on calendar management is for those that manage/lead multiple locations. It's imperative for a leader who leads multiple locations to get on the road and to be in all locations on a periodic basis. Again, leadership is not for the faint of heart, nor for those who are not committed to the needs of those he leads.

- **Change the way you walk through the building:** We have all worked in buildings with multiple entrances, with multiple elevators, and with at least 2 passageways to get to our offices from the elevator or front door. Change it up. Similar to the Manager that finds an office as far away from the people he leads as possible, we've all run across too many managers that always take "the path of least resistance," and possess the mindset, "how can I get to or from my office with having as few people as possible see me?" The Leader's objective is the opposite, on the way home the Leader is thinking, "which path can I take where I will pass by as many workstations as possible to say goodnight and thank you to as many of my players as possible."

- **Start every conversation with a "check-in:** Similar to our meeting practice to include social conversation in a meeting, each meeting with a player should start with, "how are you feeling?", "what's new", "what did your family do this weekend?" Start with a Social Conversation and then, as time and situation dictate, move onto the Performance Conversation.

- **Physical posture:** If you have ever witnessed a reluctant sales prospect, you can tell a lot from their body language. A set of folded arms across the chest is a sure sign that your message is either not getting through, or is decidedly not being received. Simply put, your intended recipient is not listening to your message. With that as a premise, now think about including your head, heart, and body in each of your conversations. If you're expressing your commitment to your players with head, heart, and body (some would say mind, body, spirit) in your social conversations, your eyes are up, you are trying to make eye contact, your body is positioned and expressing to those with whom you are speaking, that you are both present and interested. Don't ask, "How are you this morning?" then look down at your agenda – waiting for the person to stop speaking so you can get on with business. Ask, "How are you this morning," lean into the person to express your interest, and try to make eye contact – as if you care. Present evidence that you are listening by nodding your head – it is not rocket science. We are all well aware of the A-type personality that is nearly ready to burst out in a desire to get on with things or is not listening because they are formulating what they want to say next. We can temper this insidious tendency in both ourselves as well as others by intentionally practicing a more interested, physical posture during these conversations. There is no doubt that through a more active listening posture that your mind will stay more centered on the conversation and you will quickly lose these annoying habits, and soon enjoy the reputation of being a patient, involved listener, as well as a brilliant conversationalist.

There is a story about Dale Carnegie attending a fancy cocktail party many years ago. At the end of the evening, the hostess of the gala event received many compliments about Mr. Carnegie, and his skills as a brilliant conversationalist. When she inquired of him what had been the subject of a vast majority of his conversations that evening, he simply shrugged his shoulders and told her that he had simply asked open-ended questions, punctuated by additional questions such as "tell me more," and allowing the other person to continue to talk at will. Through his disciplined listening skills, he was able to establish his credentials as a brilliant, caring conversationalist. This is certainly an example that we can easily emulate with a bit of practice.

How Do I Know If They Are Really Listening?

One of the authors was on an incentive trip to stately and regal London, England, designed to honor the company's top producers from the previous year. The receiving line at a black tie dinner allowed him to test out the importance of listening, and the corollary that most people simply do not listen under most circumstances, period. Boredom, as well as the desire to test out these theories drove him to start saying inane things to those he was greeting in the formal receiving line. Borrowing yet another example from the life of President Theodore Roosevelt, the author proved his point to those he had confided his intentions.

In the case of President Roosevelt, he too was at a gala ball, and was also tired of having to field the mind numbing pleasantries of those who may have been flustered or overwhelmed from being greeted by the President of the United States. He began to greet guests with "I murdered my grandmother this morning." Most did not blink an eye or even acknowledge what he said until one keenly listening diplomat did, and responded in a whisper, "I'm sure she had it coming to her!"

So with that much of an introduction, we are certain that idle curiosity alone will prompt you to read on, and to discover what the author said in the course of his experiment. While some may be surprised, others will be dismayed to learn that with a smile on his face, a firm handshake and direct eye contact, as well as a hand on the back of the person going through the line, the author was able to utter "my grandmother wears a leather thong when she bowls," and absolutely not one person reacted in any manner so as to indicate that they had heard the remark as anything out of the ordinary. If this is frightening to you, just imagine all the really important stuff that is being missed due to inattentive listening because it is not an art that we place a great deal of premium on in this age of the text message and e-mail. Please note that the thong referred to was a wrist thong.

Conclusion

A closing note, in which we hopefully address a nagging concern, for at this point we are certain that there are some of you who might be thinking that using formal practices to have social conversations is, well, "fake." And that those we lead will easily see our actions as either insincere or some form of mockery. Others may be wondering how does a seemingly "non-caring" Manager suddenly trying to act like he cares without appearing like a fraud or as if he possesses an ulterior motive. Well, that could be the result, if the Manager is only trying to have a social conversation for his own needs. Remember, the shift from Manager to Leader is driven by a change in the focus of our attention from that of self to others. When we make this emotional shift inside and the intention of our social conversation is our care for others, then we're not faking it. And, yes, maybe our Players will need to adapt to this behavior and will need to see some level of consistency before they believe your intentions are good. In any event, we guarantee that with the right intention, the proper practice, and a consistent commitment to master this skill, you will become a far more effective communicator, and most decidedly notice others are more compelled to want to follow you and to implement the tenets of your shared vision.

Chapter 10

Resolved

The Performance Conversation

Perhaps the most difficult of all conversations to hold, regardless of the nature of the relationship between Player and Coach, is the one related to performance. Simple human nature dictates that even top performers will approach annual performance reviews with some degree of apprehension because of that old negative emotion we know as *fear*. Managers and Leaders will also often approach these meetings with some degree of trepidation even when the news they have to deliver is positive for the player! For whatever reason, we, both the Player and the Coach, do not like to quantify our Players' performance.

More than once we have referred to topics related to leadership as discussed in *Leadership and the Art of Conversation* by Kim Krisco. In this work, Krisco espouses the use of *Speech Acts* in leadership. Speech Acts consist of the use of very specific language in the art of leading and directing the performance of people in organizations. Of course Speech Acts are not something new, philosophers even as far back as the 17th century were considering how language could be used to clarify the truth; and, many of the examples used below come not only from Krisco's work, but from these early philosophical ideals. We introduce Speech Acts in a significant way here because the topic fits perfectly with the idea of performance and development based conversations.

Krisco introduces the idea of Past, Present, and Future-based conversations. If we consider a performance conversation between a Manager and subordinate as a discussion about how an assigned task has been performed, in essence we are having a past-based conversation. Past-based conversations are perfectly suited for the review of performance in that it contains evaluations of facts (what has been done). The manager then makes an assessment about those facts based on some criteria, both objective and subjective, which the manager or the company has previously established.

When we say Performance Conversations we certainly include the annual or periodic, formal assessments of performance that are utilized by companies to determine promotions, merit increases, demotions or terminations, and eligibility for advancement. But, we also refer to Performance Conversations in the context of simply providing feedback to someone about the level of performance being exhibited on any task, assignment, or request that has been made. Most certainly we think of this feedback as being passed by a manager to a subordinate; but, it also can go the other way between subordinate and manager, from manager to peer, or any direction for that matter. The Performance Conversation, the sharing of facts and an assessment about a request made, is the second conversation that the Manager, Leader, and Leader Coach need to master.

This conversation, as portrayed so far, appears one-way and stuck in the past. What makes a Performance Conversation come alive and where real-value is added for all involved is when we can turn this conversation from the past to the future. When we shift the conversation from the past to the future we then have the possibility of stepping into the Development Conversation, which we will address in detail in Chapter 11. Some would say that performance conversations can live in the future, when we shift the focus of sharing of facts and assessments from the past to what is needed in future. We would agree that if the conversation shifts to a discussion about new observations, behaviors, and approaches, with a focus on the future that it has also shifted to being a Developmental Conversation, with hints of "New Possibilities." If we observed this shift being regularly made in the marketplace today, we would not be writing this book. Unfortunately, what we do observe all too often today is the simple, managerial reiteration of the original request – which in retrospect is pretty bizarre. This technique of keeping conversations stuck in the past reminds us of the saying, "the definition of crazy is doing something over and over again the same way and expecting a different result." What we believe is that the Performance Conversation can be enhanced by adding the techniques of a Leader Coach – focusing attention more on others and focusing the player's attention on "New Possibilities."

How do we make this shift in technique? Well, let's talk about what doesn't work first and reposition those issues into what will work great. Some of the critical issues we observe include:

- **Poor preparation:** A great performance conversation starts with two elements, the initial request (discussed below) and preparation. It amazes and embarrasses both of us when we hear stories of annual appraisals being conducted and written where managers have: never written up an appraisal, let their subordinate write their own appraisal[2], or never have an end of period discussion about performance. As we shared in chapters 2 and 6, leading people is a sacred responsibility. By not handling these discussions seriously certainly means the manager is solely focused on himself (not on others), and therefore falls far short of the mark in terms of being a leader. Regardless of whether a discussion is an end of year appraisal or a quick weekly check in, the Manager, Leader, or Leader Coach is well advised to prepare for a conversation where performance feedback is to be provided. And, since we encourage providing this feedback at every opportunity, preparation is key for each of these interactive sessions. Why prepare? Because the people you have been entrusted to lead and to provide stewardship deserve nothing less. The key to any performance discussion starts with the sharing of appreciative inquiry. What is appreciative inquiry? In the context of leading people, we

---

[2] Self-appraisals. Self-appraisals are great tools that we both avidly support. Conceptually, we expect our players to submit self-appraisals in contributing to periodic performance discussions. In this example we are speaking of managers that take the player's self-appraisal and put their name on, maybe taking the time to change appraisal ratings if the player has added them.

believe it's the sharing of what's right with the contributions of those that work for us. In the words of its originator, Dr. David L. Cooperrider of Case Western Reserve University, appreciative inquiry asks us to pay special attention to "the best of the past and present". So, we believe that every interaction with the players to whom we are entrusted to lead should start with heart-felt and well-considered appreciative inquiry. Nothing's more hollow than the, "you're doing great," answer to a player asking, "how am I doing?" What exactly about the player's performance is that outstanding so as to earn the label of great? Can it be replicated? What impact did his contributions have on you, your ability to lead, the ability of his peers to contribute, or to the attainment of team goals? Be prepared to share how you truly believe the player is doing, and how you would both measure and characterize his performance. Be prepared to share rich, behavioral examples of how the player's performance is hitting the target (or not hitting the target). Then be prepared with the basis for a Performance Conversation: have your facts straight; know whether a specific request was met, and if not, why it has not been met. What behaviors were observed in completing the request, what behaviors would you like to see exhibited? These are the facts and assessments that will make the Performance Conversation far more meaningful for both player and coach.

- **Failure to set expectations:** We will examine this issue in greater detail next in the "Requests" section, but the root of many performance issues is that the manager's performance expectations were never clearly identified for the player at the onset. In essence the player is flying blind. Because of this, the Player has no idea of what would meet the Manager's expectation, or who they should involve in solving an issue. Nor do they have any concept of the coach's expectations in terms of time.
- **Surprises:** The issue with sharing feedback or having performance discussions intermittently is that the player has to guess at his or her level of performance. Intermittent performance discussions can lead to one of two issues. One, the player feels their performance isn't hitting the mark and

must assume that their performance is failing – leading to low morale and disengagement. Two, the player has a false sense of confidence in their performance and when he or she receives feedback that their performance is not meeting expectations, he or she is rightfully angry and probably will suffer low morale and engagement. So you see, either way, not having performance conversations is a lose-lose for all involved.

- **Lack of involvement:** In essence this is somewhat of a repeat of the themes above, but slightly different. In Michael Gerber's best-selling book on entrepreneurship, *The E-Myth Revisited,* he discusses one of the common failures of entrepreneurs possessing poor management skills. Entrepreneurs making the shift from small business person, focused on the technical skills inherent to their start up business, fail to make the shift to manager of people and processes. These quickly growing businesses have difficulty when the entrepreneur manages by abdication rather than management by delegation. Meaning that in assigning new responsibilities to those we manage, we mistakenly drop an assignment on a player without explaining how we want a process or assignment to be completed. Managers need to ensure that when they place a highly talented resource on an assignment they stay involved, not from a micromanaging perspective (nothing will scare off a high performer faster), but from an involved and interested perspective. Again, we contrast between coaching from the sidelines or from within the game as a Leader Coach.

- **Poor time management or investment of time:** Again, this speaks to our preparation responsibility. When we manage our time poorly, we run from meeting to meeting without thought to the intention of the meeting. Invariably, the player gets caught up in this vicious cycle; working for a manager that intermittently drops in and out, without ever spending real time with the player. Just as we spoke to the need for Presence in Chapter 7, the Manager, Leader, or Leader Coach needs to use these presence techniques for the performance conversation.

Since we believe that it is important to share best practices, we want to share a successful method that Don has used several times over the years to make the performance discussion far more meaningful for both parties.

> Years ago, the Army utilized an annual efficiency report for the non-commissioned officers that prompted their leaders to rate them on a scale of 1 to 5 in 25 key areas, thus making 125 a 'perfect' score. As you might expect, this system soon was compromised due to inflation being utilized by commanders ostensibly to help their players get ahead of their peers insofar as promotions boards, assignments, and duty stations were concerned. Unfortunately this prompted a backlash when an *honest* rating might have a detrimental impact on a soldier's career.
>
> Another shortcoming of this system is that it was an *annual* report that did not require interim feedback to the rated soldier. It also put a tremendous burden on the entire rating chain, because it forced them to capsulate an entire year's performance into a single report done in the sterile environment of their office.
>
> Don's solution was to take two of these double-sided reporting forms, laminate each of them, and armed with a pair of erasable grease pencils, conduct quarterly review sessions with each of his NCOs, during which each of them would rate the NCO's performance over the past quarter. A review of the numeric scores would then prompt a discussion of all the positive and negative behaviors and performances, and lay the foundation for a future goals discussion. It also provided Don with valuable, timely, and reliable input for the annual report. More importantly, the individual soldier, as well as the entire unit, benefited from this exchange because he had instantaneous feedback on his performance. Don used this in several different command assignments, and years later, as a sales leader, devised a numeric rating sheet solely to replicate this same experience for his district managers. The resulting discussions were of tremendous value with the very same results. It worked each and every time. *Try it, or your money back!*

> **Key Learnings:**
>
> - People are always their own harshest critic, and will inevitably rate themselves far more critically and severely than you do as a Leader Coach.
> - That being said, your score is undoubtedly going to be higher than their own evaluation, which is going to make them believe that you see them in a much better light than they see themselves. Thus the seeds of love are planted.
> - This disparity in their favor will make them more receptive to your comments and observations as a coach because they will not begin the conversation in a defensive posture. In other words, you can say just about anything that you want to say to them, and they are going to be far more receptive than they would otherwise have been.

PERFORMANCE STARTS WITH REQUESTS

As discussed above (in Failure to Set Expectations), Performance Conversations can be non-starters based on a misunderstanding of what was expected of the player in the first place. Great performance-based conversations start with the original request. The original request needs to be very specific and should outline for those to whom we are making the request what we are looking for, when we want it, with whom they should work, and what resources they should use. Trouble starts when we are not specific enough with our requests. Requests that go wrong typically head down this path because managers generally have not thought through what they need. Leaders' needs are more thoughtful – getting so specific that they define their conditions of satisfaction. If a manager or leader is not getting the desired performance from one of their players, the first consideration should be, "am I making proper requests?" It's only after we've considered the quality of our request that we should shift to considering the quality of the work of our player.

After we have gotten specific with our requests, we need to make it habitual. Persistence and consistency are great leader qualities – ensuring we reinforce high performance again and again by the way we make requests not only shows great leadership, but will also guarantee high performance.

We have previously discussed the value of preparing for Performance Conversations and conducting these conversations consistently. For the remainder of the chapter we will discuss how the Manager, Leader, and Leader Coach differ in their approach and style in having these conversations.

Manager Approach

As we discussed in Chapter 1, we see the Manager as having mastered the basic, administrative responsibilities for assessing performance and sharing that assessment with the player. There's no escaping it, this is part of the basic requirement of being a Manager. The great Manager will ensure that these conversations are taking place on a regular basis. One of the best, basic compliments a Manager can receive is, "you always know where you stand with him." At times this is where the compliment ends or can serve as the basis for additional compliments, which is great. Unfortunately it can many times be followed up with a pejorative comment like, "he only cares about himself," or "he's only interested in getting to the next level." These are the types of comments that would indicate the Manager is taking care of the managerial responsibilities of the role, but has not stepped into leadership – his attention is clearly self serving and not on others.

Again, we see the basics for good, managerial performance conversations as:

- **Make a well-considered request:** Again, strong performance and therefore favorable Performance Conversations start with a strong request. The strength and specificity of the request many times will lead to the strength and quality of the deliverable. The request should be specific, stating what you would like, when you would like it, and with what resources you'd expect something to be completed. If you as the manager have a very strong preference for the manner in which something should be done, it is incumbent upon you to share that with your player. Many times we as leaders have a highly preferred manner in which we would like work to be done, yet, we don't want to assume the appearance of micro-managers. Our players return again and again with what they believe is the desired result only to be turned away – another swing and miss. Nothing can demoralize and disengage a player faster than being told time and time again that they are not hitting the mark, when quite frankly they are delivering everything that was asked of them, or worse, they simply don't know what the desired target is! If you as a manager have a strongly desired approach, share it!

- **Prepare:** As we discussed in chapter 7, many times we need to prepare to be present. Well, we most certainly need to offer the same preparation for Performance Conversations. In preparing for Performance Conversations, we should review the requests that have been made – hopefully you've noted these requests in some file that captures what was requested and when you expected it. Also, in this file are the previous interim status reports provided, which can serve as good reference material for more formal appraisal–based, Performance Conversations. Part of preparation will be the management of time (discussed next), ensuring that time is set aside to prepare.

- **Manage your time:** Managing time refers to a number of things to keep track of, the first of which is frequency. Our people deserve our time. There can be no working relationship, and certainly no leadership, in the absence of time together. Have you ever worked for someone where you simply never saw or heard from the person?

> **Learning:** Unless the boss is giving you a wide range of latitude out of respect, trying to *guess* what the boss wants can be incredibly frustrating as well as very unproductive for all involved. However, take the example of Don's boss when he first became a Regional Sales Manager. They actually went seven weeks without any one-on-one contact, and it occurred only after Don reached out in an effort to "check in." This "check in" occurred because Don was incredibly bored on his weekly commute from Cincinnati back to Chicago, and needed someone to talk to in order to while away the miles up I-65. Imagine his surprise when he was told, "I hired you because I knew that you had a vision, a plan, and that you knew what had to be done. The last thing you needed was to have me in your hair or back pocket."
>
> **Learning:** Another friend who is now the President of his own venture said to Don over lunch the other day, "when I was younger, I used to resent the direction that I was receiving on what seemed like a constant basis. Now, that it all starts and stops with me, I would *welcome* some direction."

Granted, with the many marvels of modern communications and telecommuting that takes place today, it's quite common for people who work together to never see each other face to face. That's not what we're talking about here. What we are discussing is the need to be intentional about investing time to connect, be it in person or by phone – let's not relegate this relationship to e-mail (which our society has so ineptly fostered). The second item to manage is time to prepare (as discussed above), and the third is consistency. We may manage our calendars with the best of intention to spend time with those we lead, and before we know it, we're running around frenetically. Leading through those we lead is where our results and satisfaction will ultimately come. Show your commitment to that value by persistently and consistently honoring the time and preparation for these conversations.

- **Open with a Social Conversation and Appreciative Inquiry:** It may seem programmed or clichéd, but there's no reason to start any interaction with corrective feedback. Every person deserves the respect of a greeting and the acknowledgement of their worth and value as a human. This quick check in also allows the manager to ensure this is an appropriate time for the player to receive feedback. Plain and simply there are times when the players we lead may not be prepared emotionally for a Performance Conversation – just as we may not be prepared. In these circumstances, it's best just to reschedule time for the conversation or use the time for other purposes. We're all too busy to spend time that amounts to effectively "pushing a rope." If the time's not right for a Performance Conversation, don't go there.
- **Share specific examples (facts and assessments):** Finally, share what needs to be shared about the player's performance. What has met or exceeded the expectations of the initial request? What behaviors were exhibited when completing the request? What was expected, what was delivered? If expectations were not met, how did they fall short? What behaviors were exhibited that prevented expectations from being met?

The number of books written on this topic are too numerous to count, but the important thing is that we share what we're thinking in a straight forward way, focused on expectations and behaviors. We keep our feelings out of the conversation and we respect the feelings of those we're conversing with. We've assessed ahead of time (through preparation) how we feel the conversation will be received emotionally. We've determined how those emotions will impact the player's ability to listen and contribute to the conversation. We've also realistically determined that the conversation may need to take place over multiple interactions, by assessing how much information can be shared and accepted in a single interaction.

At this point the manager has done the job. Performance Conversations are taking place on a regular basis, both formally and informally. The Manager is preparing properly and is sharing facts and assessments about the status of requests that have been made in the past. The question now is how do we enhance those conversations? How do we make them richer, potentially less contentious, and more productive (by enhancing performance and engagement going forward)? We take a Leader approach – an approach that shifts the attention of our focus more from self to others.

LEADER APPROACH

So how would the leader approach differ than the managerial approach? Take two atta boys out of petty cash if you guessed that it would be by focusing the attention of the conversation squarely on the player rather than on yourself. Ah, you ask, isn't the entire conversation focused on the player already; aren't we talking about the player's performance? Yes, we are, but at this point it is solely in the context of the request made by the manager, and how well the manager's needs are being met. The leader approach will shift the conversation to the needs of the player, and allow the magic and art of leadership to come shining through.

The first change the leader will make is the more liberal use of appreciative inquiry - providing real, reinforcing feedback that captures the head, heart, and body of the player. This appreciative inquiry is well thought through, and shares the essence of why their contribution is important to the player, the leader, as well as to the organization. Leaders also use appreciative inquiry to redirect a player's existing strength into an area that has not been as strong for the player in the past. For example, we may have a player that builds relationships well, partners with other team members, and expertly involves stakeholders in conversations and decisions, yet has a shortcoming in the ability to analyze data or problem-solve. We are reasonably confident that there is probably also someone on your team that's diametrically opposed in strengths and weaknesses. This person may be a whiz kid, yet alienates all of his work partners due to personality issues. This is the perfect opportunity for the powerhouse relationship builder to partner with the whiz kid, and ideally, for them to help one another turn weaknesses into strengths. The manner in which this would come to pass is through the Performance Conversation.

In the Performance Conversation, right after focusing on the positive feedback regarding the player's ability to interact, we would then encourage him to redirect that skill in partnership with another so as to turn his heretofore previous weakness into a newfound strength. This is by definition a true win-win approach because both players receive reinforcing feedback about a strength, which further engages them; and, this strength is then directed on an area which needs to be developed. By having each player take a skill with which he is comfortable and apply it in an area to develop, the company gains the benefits of increasing performance two-fold.

When leaders have Performance Conversations, they are able to move the conversation from a simple sharing of facts and assessments, a past-based conversation, to a conversation of the present. This shift in conversation comes from the leader's ability to connect the player's contributions to the Vision and Mission of the organization. And, in making this connection for the player, the leader engages them to participate in the super ordinate goal of the organization, making them feel that "my contribution helps and matters." It is this connection to the mission of the team, where the leader is able to connect the player's performance, both positive and negative, and to engage them to contribute their "discretionary effort".

A side note on "discretionary effort." Discretionary effort is the "other 25%" of effort that each of us can contribute to our respective organizations. It is given only when we are engaged and compelled to offer it. What is this "other 25%", and how does it come about? We all can get by and meet the expectations of our roles by giving the basic 75%. When we give the basic 75%, we offer what's needed to meet the expectations of the role we play, no more, no less. Yet, each of us has a reserve tank, the "other 25%," that we can choose to use or not use, because it truly is at our discretion (thus discretionary effort). Who can compel others to give their discretionary effort? Leaders can. Why? Because it is a fact that players are compelled to follow great leaders, and will be willing to offer their discretionary effort. How do leaders compel others to want to follow, to want to give their discretionary effort? If you guessed that it is by focusing their attention on others, you are at the head of the class.

The last thing we'll offer about the Leader approach to Performance Conversations is the quality of their requests. We mentioned in the managerial approach that the basis for great performance starts with a quality request from the manager. We also shared that these requests should be very specific, highlighting expectations of when, where, and what should be done. Leaders take the details of requests a step further and address specifics as they relate to development, as well as conditions of satisfaction. When leaders consider the conditions of satisfaction for a request, they consider the factors and expectations that will truly please both them, and the organization, if met. In getting this specific, the leader adds greater assurance that expectations can and will be met; and that his player will be successful – that's shifting one's attention to another. Key learning: being concerned about their success enough so as to make your requests as specific as possible will pay large dividends for one and all.

Leader Coach Approach

The Leader Coach approach differs in two primary ways. First, the Leader Coach approach focuses on the player actively participating in the request, assessment, and correction of performance; and, second, the Leader Coach approach makes a dramatic shift to future-based conversations, truly focusing on New Possibilities. The idea of future-based Developmental Conversations will be addressed in Chapter 11. For now, let's talk about the Leader Coach approach to Performance Conversations.

Think about the typical Performance Conversation you have had with your players in the past or that you have had with your boss. In essence one could generally classify these conversations as mentoring conversations. These conversations generally consist of the sharing of facts and assessments and the boss's idea for redirecting effort to improve in the future. In essence these conversations follow the typical Manager/Leader to Player format of being directive, or the boss telling the subordinate what to do. We see the Leader Coach approach as being dramatically different. These conversations are not directive, but consultative. As the lawyer among us (Don) would say, "the Leader Coach approach uses the Socratic Method." Of course Terry had to look up the meaning of Socratic Method, but after understanding the meaning, he'd say Don is using a fancy word for the Coaching Method. In short, regardless of whether we call it the Socratic Method or the

Coaching method, it is "teaching by asking rather than telling." In this non-directive manner of managing performance, the Leader Coach uses questioning to guide the player through problem-solving. Certainly, there will be times when the Leader Coach needs to make a managerial assessment of performance (back to the foundation), but it is in the redirecting, correcting, and reinforcement part of the Performance Conversation that the Leader Coach can use the Socratic Method to correct/improve performance. Having both been leaders for 25 years, this is easier said than done. Each of us has developed habits about the way we manage performance and conduct Performance Conversations. We, like most leaders, have been quite successful telling (directing) performance as Leaders; and when you've been successful in the past it's not easy to the shift from this Leader approach to a Leader Coach approach. First, the Leader Coach model will require new habits and some practice. Second, the Leader Coach approach requires more emotional energy, preparation, and awareness in order to reinforce the coaching model rather than slipping into the directive model.

How does a Leader Coach approach Performance Conversation sound? As we did for our Social Conversation, let's use an example, and return to Jim and Sarah.

KNOCK, KNOCK, KNOCK (at Sarah's office door)

"Hi Jim, what's up?" asks Sarah.

"Can I talk to you a bit about my cost per call metric? I know I haven't met goal the past 2 weeks and was curious if you could help me identify some areas for improvement?" asks Jim.

"I'd be happy to help. I've been monitoring the reports for the past few weeks, and have noticed on your reports that your average talk time per call has been 60 seconds higher than most of the other teams," notes Sarah.

"I've noticed that too, but did not think that was a key driver of the cost," replies Jim.

"Well all of your other metrics that go into cost have been at target, so that would be the first place I would look. Why don't you take a detailed look at the impact of that metric and then get back to me," offers Sarah.

"Will do, I will follow up with you tomorrow."

Pretty productive conversation; Jim had a problem and he discussed it with Sarah. They arrived at a potential solution and Jim is off and running. How could this conversation be different?

First, start with a social conversation and appreciative inquiry! Then don't tell, ask! Let's see how the Leader Coach might approach this conversation.

KNOCK, KNOCK, KNOCK (at Sarah's office door)

"Hi Jim, what's up?" asks Sarah.

[We are skipping the Social Conversation. If you want to review it, go back to Chapter 9.]

"Can I talk to you a bit about my cost per call metric? I know I haven't met goal the past 2 weeks and was curious if you could help me identify some areas for improvement?" asks Jim.

"First Jim, I want to share with you that I know you're working on cost per call and I appreciate it. I also appreciate you approaching me to ask for help; I consider that a great trait. Although I know you're working on cost per call, I wanted you to know that I appreciate the high morale of your team. When your team operates at this level it helps to set an example for all of the other teams, and that will improve the performance of the entire department. Nicely done. Now, I'd be happy to help on this cost issue. What have you noticed in your call metric reports lately?" asks Sarah.

"Well, I have been reviewing them and really haven't seen anything that I thought would be a key driver," states Jim.

"Okay, you've made your assessment, but tell me what did you *see* that led you to make that assessment?" persists Sarah.

"Well I did notice my talk time was about 60 seconds higher than the standard," says Jim.

"What else did you see?" asks Sarah.

"I really didn't see any other change in the metrics," says Jim.

"Nice job holding your other key metrics steady, what led you to believe that talk time did not have an impact on cost?" asks Sarah.

"Well, it just doesn't seem that talk time being that high would have that dramatic an impact," says Jim.

> "What's the calculation you're using to determine your cost per call? Why don't you show me how the metrics interplay here to determine the cost per call," questions Sarah.
>
> [JIM MAPS OUT HIS EQUATIONS FOR SARAH.]
>
> "Jim, you've absolutely got the interplay of metrics down pat. Now, how might you understand the impact of the two different levels of performance?" asks Sarah.
>
> "Well, I could calculate the cost using the two different levels of performance," says Jim.
>
> "Great, let's go ahead and try that," encourages Sarah.
>
> [JIM CALCULATES COST BOTH WAYS.]
>
> "Wow, I guess I didn't believe the cost could be impacted that much by such a small shift in the metric," offers Jim.
>
> "Okay, so we've gotten this far by comparing methodologies. What might you try different the next time you run across something like this?" asks Sarah.
>
> "Guess, I shouldn't be so quick to make an assessment without proving it to myself," states Jim.
>
> "You've got it Jim. Nice piece of work and learning. Anything else I can help you with?" asks Sarah.
>
> "No, I think I'm all set. I appreciate your help, I really learned something," says Jim.
>
> "You taught yourself, I just asked. Oh, and by the way, thanks again for the morale of your team and your leadership. Maybe you could connect with your teammates and ask them a few questions about how they're handling costs, and share with them what you are doing to keep morale so high," states Sarah.

How does Jim feel? Well, after the first conversation he leaves Sarah's office feeling that she's the expert, and really doesn't get anything but an answer to his question. Maybe he feels a bit smaller than Sarah, as he needs to go to her to solve his problems. After the second conversation, Sarah has made Jim feel like an expert on managing morale; and although his team might not be hitting on all cylinders, they're still making a great contribution – he's the expert in that area. Second,

Jim solved his own problem regarding costs, and walked away from the conversation with the tools necessary to potentially solve his own challenges in the future. In fact, we guarantee that when Jim runs across a similar issue, he will solve the problem and will be chomping at the bit to show Sarah how he went about solving the problem himself. Lastly, he walked away with some helpful feedback about the behaviors he exhibited in the way he approached the problem initially and has some ideas on how to exhibit a different set of behaviors next time – a new practice.

What else did you notice about the conversation? Sarah pretty well ends each response with a question. We'll get into questioning more in Chapter 11, but suffice is to say, questioning is the primary tool of the Leader Coach.

One key learning about questioning before we move on; please note that every question Sarah asked starts with the word, "what." "What" is a great way to initiate a question because it eliminates judgment and assessment. Imagine if the questions started with the word "why." For example, "why didn't you think that talk time would impact cost?" There's a loaded question. Sarah might just well have called Jim a knucklehead.

What's needed to take the Leader Coach approach?

Look at that, a "what" question. We'll answer this one for you.

- **Curiosity:** The Leader Coach needs to get curious. What's driving the player to think this way? What was the approach taken? How can I structure a question to help guide the player? Is there something to be learned by me in this approach? What am I missing? When we put ourselves in the state of curiosity we are open to learning new skills, learning something new about the players we lead, learning a different approach to problem solving, and learning something new about ourselves.
- **Acceptance/flexibility:** First we need to accept our role and accept our worth to ourselves and the organization – more on this below. But, we also must accept our player's perspective and consider it as right before we react. At this

point flexibility is the key. We need to be flexible enough to consider that there may be more than one right answer to the question or problem being reviewed. And, we should be flexible enough to allow for an alternative solution if it achieves our end result.

- **Patience:** This is tough for Terry (and sometimes for Don too). He likes to see results, check it off the list, and move on to the next item. That approach does not work here, because the goal in these circumstances is not just getting the job done, but also developing a future leader. It's back to the, "teach a man to fish" idea.
- **Letting go of ego:** As a Leader Coach we need to feel comfortable handing control to someone else, and letting others shine while we take a back seat. We need to learn how to enjoy and find fulfillment from seeing others achieve, and genuinely experiencing self-actualization. This occurs when we allow someone else other than ourselves to enjoy basking in the spot light. Boldness, caused by a need to assert our strength, often leads to an attempt to steal it from others, and needs to be avoided.
- **Confidence in yourself:** It might seem a bit dramatic, but the Leader Coach must possess a righteous intent as he approaches the coaching session. When we take the Leader Coach approach, we will never need to second guess ourselves about why we are coaching the player - it's never to belittle them, or to make the player look smaller. It certainly is never to make ourselves look bigger. When we take a coaching approach with the player, this righteous intent will come through for both the player and those with whom the player will interact.
- **Confidence in your player:** To take a coaching approach to leadership requires us to see our players as inherently gifted and capable of much more than they're currently taking responsibility for delivering. As a Leader Coach, it is up to us to take an inherent view that we are all capable of greatness. This view of all people as inherently talented relieves a great deal of tension within an organization. First,

the leader needs to view his own skills in this manner. In this way, there is neither jealousy nor intimidation in allowing our players to take on some of our own responsibilities. Our goal is to coach them, while finding our satisfaction in doing so. When we take this approach, we make room for our players to grow. We then have the capacity to grow ourselves, looking at "New Possibilities" made available to us by our boss, the organization, or other interests we may have discovered. What a great win-win! With this confidence that we are all gifted masterpieces of our creator, there is less concern that a player is taking over our responsibilities or that we're being "passed" by another. This will require us to revel in our own beauty so that we can more easily revel in the beauty of others. As Denis Waitley said in his book, Seeds of Greatness, "we must feel love inside ourselves before we can give it to others." There is an anonymous adage that states "a candle loses nothing by lighting another candle."

BENEFITS OF THE LEADER COACH APPROACH

Some of you may actually be contemplating the sheer effort associated with being a Leader Coach, and feeling a bit overwhelmed. If so, relax, this is normal. Just like anything else, at first it takes practice, and it might take longer to get something done; but, we are talking about making an investment here, and creating future assets for our organization. In Robert Kiyosaki's best selling books based on *Rich Dad, Poor Dad*, he defines an asset as anything that produces future cash flow. That's just what we are doing with the Leader Coach approach. We are helping our players make contributions in the future without us there. If we simply answer the question or solve the problem, and our players need to come back to us every time they have an issue, we have not created the desired asset. The benefits of the Leader Coach approach include:

- **Lowers the dependency on the Leader:** As we shared above, by using a Leader Coach approach we teach our players how to address their own needs.

- **Expands the ideas and "right solutions" being used:** As shared above, by using the Coach approach to problem solving we use questions rather than answers. If we answer the question, the solutions are only as good as our current body of knowledge. By asking questions, we provide the opportunity to learn something new, to find other right answers.
- **Improves morale and engagement of our players:** One of the largest benefits to the Leader Coach approach is the impact we have on our players. As they grow, develop new competencies, find the enjoyment in addressing their own needs, and find new confidence, the level of engagement they have for their job and their place in life grows. With a highly motivated, engaged player we capture the benefit of their discretionary effort – the other 25%.
- **Allows our leaders to live in the question, waiting for a better "right" answer:** As we sharpen our skills as a Leader Coach, we develop greater patience and flexibility. This ability to wait, to not react instinctively, provides for an environment where the next, better, right answer can appear. Too often the "shoot from the hip" answer and mindset closes off the opportunity for expanded thinking.
- **Provides an infinite amount of value:** The Manager or Leader approach is a zero sum game. The coaching approach opens up an infinite supply of ideas and energy. As Krisco shared, traditionally the leader's need to be right is an instinctual one, passed to us millions of years ago when survival depended on it – we need to let go of being right, we need to let go of our egos – only when we let our egos go will we be comfortable enough to let others be right. And, when we let others be right, the amount of potential value to be added is infinite.
- **Pay it forward:** By letting go of our egos, we help our players let go of their egos. With our egos out of the picture, we're all more open to being wrong and more willing to have future-based conversations. Within future-based conversations we open "New Possibilities." Within "New

Possibilities" we teach our players to be Leader Coaches, thus perpetuating the cycle. And, as we perpetuate the role of Leader Coach, we are Paying it Forward. We pay forward our contributions to our organizations, families, and society.

Conclusion

The Performance Conversation is the second conversation that must be mastered by the Manager, Leader, and Leader Coach. There is ever-increasing value to be added by approaching the Performance Conversation using the Leader Coach approach. In addition to the value of developing stronger players for the future, the organization wins by developing a broader, more diverse set of solutions to its business problems. Lastly, the Leader Coach wins and grows by dramatically expanding the contribution to the organization as well as to our collective existence – let's not forget these skills can and should be taken home. Think of the contribution we can make to our families and communities when we take the Leader Coach approach in all we do. Now *that's* a win-win.

CHAPTER 11

Evolved

THE DEVELOPMENTAL CONVERSATION

It has all come down to this, the Developmental Conversation. We won't spend a great deal of time defining the different approaches between the Manager, Leader, and Leader Coach. The reason: the Developmental Conversation is the exclusive domain of the Leader Coach. This is where the Leader Coach flourishes, adding exponential value to an organization by increasing the value of its most important asset, its people.

One such Leader Coach is Rick Pitino, head basketball coach for the Kentucky Wildcats. As a coach of a nationally ranked athletic program, it would be easy for him to be concerned about the view from "ten thousand feet" and to leave the day-to-day coaching aspects of handling players to his assistants. But he doesn't do that. Rather, he makes it a point to use the brutal candor and honesty that is a large part of his *character* to personally learn his players' strengths and weaknesses, and to conduct regular one-on-one developmental discussion with them while utilizing a limited number of "tools" to make these conversations relevant, and relationship enhancing.

One such tool, and one that we have both used with our own children, is to establish standards (desired behaviors and practices to exhibit those behaviors), and to then simply *expect* the players to achieve these standards. When they don't, as a coach it is okay for us to express our disappointment, but in a positive way. Not in a Bobby Knight explosion of fury, but rather in unspoken words, and sometimes, merely a look with our eyes is sufficient. The single largest club that Don's father had to exact performance when Don was growing up was four simple words: "I'm disappointed in you." The key to utilizing this system effectively is the establishment of very clear and attainable goals for the player, and to establish an infrastructure of coaching and support that enables the player to achieve the standard. The standards have to be mutually agreed upon, and desired by both the coach and the player.

DEVELOPMENTAL CONVERSATIONS WITH THE MANAGER OR LEADER

For the leader and manager, the Developmental Conversation is focused on *how* the player has completed a request. This is a continuation of the Performance Conversation, where the manager's conversation was past-based, sharing facts and assessing the results the player has achieved. If we leave the conversation here, we've completed the administrative responsibility of the manager. Sure, maybe we share our assessment of the player's competencies, providing a snap shot to the player on the skills used to achieve his result; but, again the assessment of competencies is focused on the past and what was exhibited. The sharing of behaviors exhibited is certainly of value to the player, but too often this is where the conversation ends. It requires the player to determine what behavior *should* have been exhibited, and requires the player to determine, seemingly on his own, how he might muster up the strength to exhibit this different behavior in the future. That's where the leader steps in. We admire the leader's skills to move a conversation from a past-based Performance Conversation to a present-based, pseudo Developmental Conversation. In this present-based conversation, the leader shares with the player the behaviors he believes are needed to achieve expected results and which will align the player's behaviors with the values of the organization. The sharing of expected behaviors is helpful to the player, in that, it provides a picture that the player can target in the future. It does not explain *how* the player might go about overcoming the challenges associated with exhibiting these behaviors.

The Shortcoming with Today's Performance (Developmental) Systems

Where even the most advanced people development companies fail today is that they pride themselves on the huge investments in their performance management systems and believe that these systems will also address development. These systems include processes for continual feedback, having interim performance check ins, putting tremendous amounts of time into 360 feedback mechanisms (collection and sharing tools), and calibrating final results assessments across appraising managers. These tools work marvelously well in sharing facts and assessments with players (supporting past-based conversations), but do little to inform the player how to improve future performance (adding future value to the organization), which is where the real gold lies. So kudos to these few companies that make this investment in assessing past performance, but as Clara Peller shared in Wendy's 1980's commercials, "where's the beef?" The beef, the value, is how we attain even higher performance and player engagement in the future, and that is where the Leader Coach adds value by having rich Developmental Conversations.

To Be or Not To Be

Before we get into the definition of the Developmental Conversation and how to approach it, we should first consider when it's appropriate. Not all circumstances or players will be well served through a significant amount of coaching. Nor, will the leader coach want to make this high investment of time and energy with every player. For some players, leaving the player's development focused on the Performance Conversation (see Chapter 10) would be far more appropriate when the player is in the early stages of a new role and simply trying to achieve basic results. Even if the player has some degree of tenure in the role, but is still not achieving performance expectations, again it may best serve the Leader Coach-Player relationship to leave things in the realm of Performance Conversations. Recall the Stroul Learning Curve model from chapter 2, shown here as Figure 11.1. In the early tenure of the learning cycle the player's focus needs to be squarely on results - attaining the base level requirements of the role.

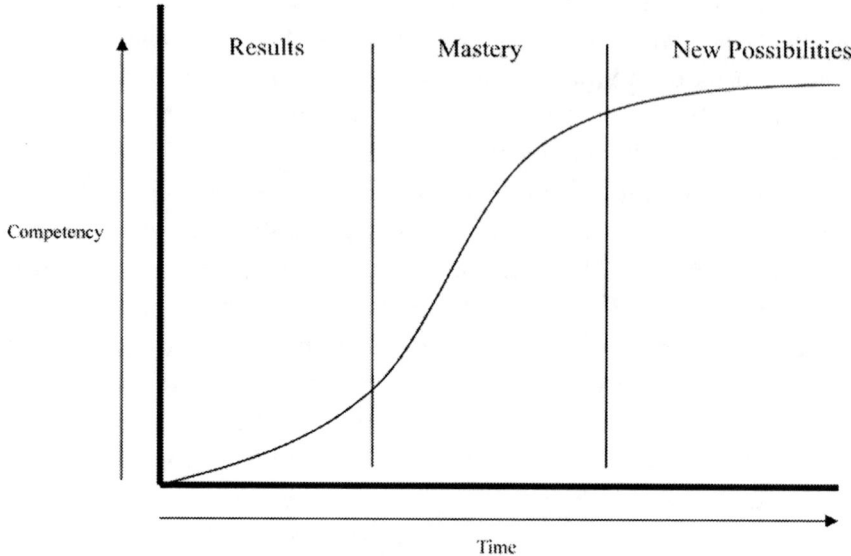

Figure 11.1

This is a good 'rule of thumb' guideline for assessing when to invest in the Development Conversation, but the Leader Coach may also want to assess, in some circumstances, why the desired result is not being achieved. If it's tenure based, or a simple learning curve issue, follow the rule of thumb. But, there may also be circumstances where the desired result is not being achieved as a by-product of the player's unwillingness to work at their development or towards the needed results. As we will discuss below, this may be caused by a misalignment of values between the player and the organization. The simple two-by-two matrix below, Figure 11.2 is a well-known model termed, "Willing and Able."

Willing and Able Model

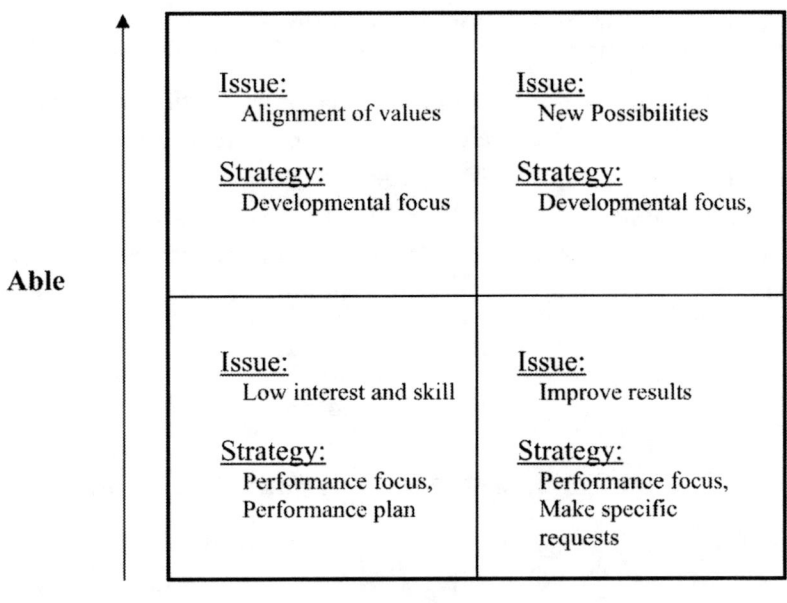

Figure 11.2

In the high "willing" and high "able" quadrant, we have a high performing player that is fully engaged. This is a perfect candidate for coaching and full engagement in the Developmental Conversation, as this candidate is most likely ready to uncover "New Possibilities." Conversely, the player in the low "willing" and low "able" quadrant may be a performer where the Leader Coach keeps the conversation solely focused on performance and attaining base level results with little energy invested in development conversation. The key then is the remaining two quadrants. The first, high "able" and low "willing" is the perfect candidate for a Development Conversation. This player may benefit from coaching and developmental conversations focused on aligning his values with the organization, and therefore more fully engaging the player in the future. In the other quadrant, we have a fully engaged player, high "willing," who has not yet attained full performance potential. In this quadrant, we may want to offer some coaching, yet the focus should remain on the performance conversation. Please refer to chapter 10 for guidance with the Performance Conversation.

Simply put, there will be players who are incredibly willing, but not able to perform at the level deemed necessary by the organization. Do we jettison them? Absolutely not. It may mean reassignment, retraining, or some other change. By the same token, we may have a player who is more than able, but not willing. This is a horse of an entirely different color. Each situation has to be approached on a case by case basis, and may present some of the most challenging and/or rewarding coaching experiences.

With these thoughts firmly fixed in your mind, you are now ready to enter the world of coaching, so read on.

THE DEVELOPMENTAL CONVERSATION DEFINED

The Developmental Conversation is all about discovering and implementing "New Possibilities." It's expansive, soulful, and exciting; yet, scary enough to command our respect. Whitworth, Kimsey-House, and Sandahl, in their book *Co-Active Coaching*, describe the coach's role as helping players to define their values and then assisting them to live within them.

Helping our players to live within their values helps them in "being fulfilled," and completely within the pursuit of purpose. This is different than the state of "having fulfillment," where an achievement is recognized. An achievement, such as receiving positive feedback about a result, is great, but also quite fleeting – it is only momentary gratification. Therefore we equate "having fulfillment" with Performance Conversations in which we review what we set out to do, how it was achieved, and ultimately whether it was fulfilled. This differs from the Developmental Conversation, which is the assistance provided to the player in "being fulfilled," wherein we are helping the player to step into congruence and harmony, and to ultimately live their values. To accomplish this requires the coach to recognize, appreciate, and share (expose) the soul of the player in a mutually gratifying conversation.

The Developmental Conversation necessarily is intended to stir passions and purpose, to fully engage a player's soul, and to recruit their "other 25%." When we shift the focus of the conversations from alignment with an organizationally designed goal (a performance goal) to a player's designed value (a developmental goal), we open New Possibilities for the Leader Coach-Player relationship.

As we discussed in Chapter 10, there is inevitably some degree of apprehension when we engage in performance conversations. What is the main apprehension? For most, it is the very fact that the manager is sitting in judgment of his or her player. In great Developmental Conversations, where a Leader Coach and player are discussing values, the conversation can certainly be intimidating, but the element of judgment has been removed. When the conversation focuses on the player's values and their personal development, we might be *observing*, and then sharing the observation that the player isn't hitting *their defined* mark; but because they are pursuing their values, i.e. their values, the developmental goals that they defined for themselves, corrective feedback provided by the coach can be received less defensively by the player. By working at something meaningful and by attempting to develop a new skill in a new domain, the player can get focused on the journey, the process by which a new skill is being developed, rather than being engrossed in the actual result being achieved.

Congruence in the Developmental Conversation

Ideally, we aim to align a player's values with the organization's values. For, the player's fulfillment will not come from living within the organization's values, but will come from living within their own value system. As a Leader or Leader Coach, one of our goals needs to be the development of a persuasive vision, cast into our organizations in such a manner as to "compel others to want to follow." When we can cause the values of the organization and player to align; when they are in congruence with one another; we set up the opportunity for our players to be in a state of "being fulfilled." And, once in this state, the player not only is striving to develop new skills aligned with these values, but is also willing to offer his discretionary effort (the other 25%.)

Leader Coach's Role in Aligning Values

What happens when a player's values are not aligned with those of the organization? As long as the player's base level contribution is adding value, meeting expectations, is not destructive to the team, and cannot be "traded for better talent," it should be deemed either adequate or permissible to retain the player on the team. Leaders need to be willing to accept a person's values that differs from his own or that of the organization's, and be willing to accept the player's minimal required effort if it is meeting their needs. This is where the Leader Coach must be able to separate performance from potential, and ascertain whether the player's performance is meeting expectations, and if so, insuring that this level of contribution remains in place, and continues to fulfill the needs of the organization.

To allow a player to remain within his or her own values takes a great deal of discipline and effort by the Leader Coach. Many leaders in today's environment just do not have the soulful maturity to accept that someone's values and desire to contribute are not aligned with his own. This is where the approach of the Leader Coach is more beneficial.

Do we as a Leader Coach throw our hands up and simply allow this imbalance of values between the organization, ourselves, and our players to continue without seeking change? Well sometimes we do. More often however, the Leader Coach is the one in a position to do something about alleviating this imbalance. For invariably, if there is an imbalance of values present, while the player might be meeting performance expectations, he could very well be suffering inside. It is very common for us to run across high performing players at companies that contribute well, yet behind closed doors are whining, complaining, cowering, or otherwise shouting, "this place [expletive deleted]." This is suffering. As a friend shared with us, "pain is inevitable, suffering is optional." It is one of the primary responsibilities of the Leader Coach to help players stay in balance, and to assist them in working through their suffering (thus making it optional). How do we align a player's values with those of the organization, or help them work through suffering? The answer is coaching, and by having the Developmental Conversation. In the Developmental Conversation we help our players uncover the stories they are telling themselves, or hearing about themselves from others, and in the course of these conversations, we actually assist them to re-write these stories or better yet, to create new ones.

By the way, not all misalignment or imbalance of values and goals leads to suffering on the part of players. For players that have a strong, mature awareness of their own values and goals, our goal as a Leader Coach may simply be to make ourselves available to our players and assisting them to work through this misalignment and fine tuning. In this situation we may need to get comfortable helping our player restructure their role (or find a new role) that is more aligned with their skills and values, as we indicated in the "Willing and Able" portion of this chapter. As we have heretofore shared, this will require an investment of time on the part of the Leader Coach, as well as a willingness to meet the needs of the player over our own or those of our team.

STORIES[3]

Many times a player is 'stuck' in a story about their situation. It is the role of the Leader Coach to help the player re-write the story or look for "New Possibilities." While we are decidedly not talking about changing someone's core values here, we are talking about helping the player see that their values are not as misaligned as they have led themselves to believe. In the dictionary a story is defined as a narrative or tale of real or fictitious events. In the stories we tell about ourselves and others, we cobble together a set of facts and assessments told from our own perspective in life. In these stories the facts can't change, for they are forever empirical in nature. Yet, each of us will tell a different story about the same set of facts, because each of us will make our own assessments, which will be based on our individual perspective.

Experience has also taught us that this viewing of facts from differing perspectives can also serve as the basis for many a good argument, as we can all attest to from our own brand of "constructive" discussions with our spouses. Something that Don learned as a practicing attorney is that in the routine divorce, as in any type of dispute for that matter, there are always *three* sides to every argument: his, hers, and the truth (reality), which is usually somewhere in between the first two. Both parties will

---

[3] The use of "stories" in coaching is an especially effective technique shared with Terry by Dr. Neil Stroul and taught at Georgetown University.

swear that they are telling the truth, and truly *believe* their perception to be just that; but in reality, each will present a view that is *skewed* by experience, emotion, and other external influences. The Leader Coach is trained to be aware of this tendency, and is therefore in a position to influence and assist the player with this dilemma.

When we as a Leader Coach can help players get "un-stuck" by using Developmental Conversations, we are in essence assisting them to re-write the stories that they are telling to themselves. We do so by using the Socratic Method of assistance, and forcing them to confront their own observations and to get *curious* about the assessments that *they* are making of the facts. If we can help them at least see a different assessment or perspective, then we've made available to them the concept of New Possibilities.

A "True" Story

Here's a great place for an example. While one of the authors was working for a senior executive at a major corporation, he and his peers were disgruntled with the executive. The water cooler chatter about this executive was that he was self-focused and self-serving, didn't like anyone's ideas but his own, and improperly used humor that demeaned others in the company. This guy was a "%$$@#*&" (and then some!) and we could not wait to move on, or for him to leave, but clearly, the place wasn't big enough for all of us. Of course the author prided himself on being a "people sensitive" leader, so the misalignment of values between us could not have been any more apparent. Talk about suffering. Well, through work with a coach, the author was able to get curious about what drove the senior executive's behaviors – in essence using the values of a "people sensitive" leader with the senior executive as well. By getting curious about the senior executive leader, the author was able to write a different story about him, one which portrayed him as an insecure person who did not know how to master conversation. To cover that insecurity, he used his gruff style to protect his ego. With this new story as a backdrop, he could be approached differently and more productively. By telling a different story than the one more popularly written by others, the work relationship became much more productive and collegial. By the way, by also observing the story, the author could also see his own fears and insecurities come through when this leader's style rubbed him the wrong way, which served to let him know that part of the less constructive story written about this executive was written from his own fears. It is a pretty thin pancake that does not have two sides! We owe it to ourselves, as well as our players to always consider the other possibility.

FUTURE-BASED CONVERSATION

Regardless of whether we put it in terms of misaligned values, telling stories, or what ever other model one prefers, the purpose of the Developmental Conversation is to move the player's focus from the past [and present] to that of the future. By moving the conversation from the past to the future we also move the conversation from the result(s) achieved, to a more constructive focus on the person (the player), and the possibilities associated with the future.

Of course one of the critical steps in moving our conversation from the past to the future is helping the player to *let go* of the past. While we can't ignore the past, we also can't change it. We can learn from it, but we shouldn't dwell on it.

So why is the past important to future Developmental Conversations? As we discussed in chapter 4, the set of fear-based behaviors that we may have exhibited in the past in one manner, shape, or form, may very well have contributed to the success that we have enjoyed up to this point. Secondly, the manner in which we have accomplished our work in the past is now habit and will be difficult to change without a conscious effort. We assist the player to let go of the past, by utilizing more questions that allow them to observe how the past approach may not have served them best or may not have been aligned with their values, and potentially was the root cause of their suffering (if being felt).

One effective tool to help the player move the conversation to the future is by putting observations in a category of *"up until now."* "Up until *now"* (meaning that this is as far as this is going) may be the way the player has observed, felt, or behaved; but "*from now on,*" this is the way the player intends for it to be. Using the "up until now" conversation tool helps the player let go of the past without beating themselves up because of mistakes and shortcomings previously experienced.

Too often we all get stuck in the past, because there is a need to stew over and punish ourselves mercilessly for what we perceive as shortcomings, errors, mistakes, and blunders or simply something that we have done "wrong" in the past. It's as if we are watching the character Dobby from the Harry Potter movies, beating himself in self-admonishment. What we as coaches are trying to do is to help the player get over it, put it aside, and to boldly move on.

To do this, it is incumbent upon us as a Leader Coach to subtly move the conversation, and encourage the player to let go of the past ("up until now"), and to move it to the future by utilizing the "from now on." In these latter conversations, our aim is to have the player observe that things can be different for them if *they choose* to believe it, and to map out the new future for themselves, hopefully in terms that are of benefit to both themselves and the organization. This entire concept of enabling the player to envision this new future on their own is one of the key roles of the Leader Coach during a Developmental Conversation.

Habits

A word on habits: we've all got them, some serve us well, while others may actually be a disservice, or can be down right destructive in nature. When most of us hear the word habit, we think of a set of destructive or non-productive behaviors such as nail biting, smoking, leg shaking, or swearing. A habit is actually any pattern of behaviors that has become so routine and commonplace that it is almost involuntary. When thought of in this way, we can see that the way we plan, work, or speak generally follow a habitual pattern. As a Leader Coach, we are endeavoring to assist our players identify their own habits; to determine which serve them well, and others which are a disservice and warrant change; and finally, to change those that *the player* has *declared* that they want to change. Just like changing any habit that is engrained in us, this is not necessarily going to be easy. Both the coach and player should anticipate that a bit of anger and frustration could become evident, as habits are not easily broken and when disrupting a firmly entrenched habit, that emotions can flare. Yet, one of the beautiful things about a coaching relationship is that it provides a safe environment for the player to try a new habit before it is shared with the world.

A side note on habits and assessing performance; all of us get in the habit of achieving results in a particular manner. Far too often, if players achieve expected results again and again, thus developing a long-term, tenured track record of meeting expectations, it is anticipated that advancement will follow; and far too often organizations base rewards on such a track record. We as Leader Coaches need to break this cycle, this habit. If a player's history merely reflects years of simply meeting expectation, then that's what they should be rewarded for: simply meeting expectations. The Leader Coach helps the player approach work differently, developing new habits that get the work done better, faster, cheaper or with greater impact. This new way of thinking, that of exceeding expectations, of getting the work done differently, is what should be rewarded with advancement. In the military, an officer's career choices insofar as future schooling, command opportunities, duty assignment, and most importantly promotion, are not based solely on past performance. On the contrary, an officer is selected for promotion or advancement in recognition of potential, and the ability to handle increasing levels of responsibility. While it is true that past performance should be (and is) an indicator of how an individual may perform in the new role or in duty commensurate with the new rank, this system of promotion truly is based on *potential* and New Possibilities.

Realizing and breaking old habits, and creating an organizational vision that inspires the player to establish new habits that serve their own personal vision is precisely where the Leader Coach's Developmental Conversation adds exponential value. To create these new habits we will need to assist the player see their essence, their soul, their vision for themselves that is more powerful than the temptation of the old habit. Ideally, through the art of questions, a Leader Coach can assist a player in crafting a vision of their soul in all its magnificence that is worthy of adding further energy to their ongoing effort.

Defining Success for Ourselves

One difficult habit to break that prevents us from moving forward or living within our own values is how external forces can often times negatively impact our own definition of success. All too often we allow others to define success for us rather than simply defining success for ourselves. How does this occur, and why do we allow it? The most likely answer is that we are human, and remain subject to the manner in which we are viewed by others. We see it all around us everyday.

People living by standards set by others to include the cars we drive, the homes we buy, the professions, vocations, and avocations that we choose, as well as things often beyond our control such as our physical appearance. Society adopts a prevailing view on what we should wear, or eat, or the movies we should view, and we are often forced into a position where we relinquish control of our own destiny and self image. Unfortunately, all of these external influences can have a detrimental impact on the manner in which we look ourselves in the mirror and measure our own level of success. One of the outcomes of healthy developmental or coaching conversations is the identification of the player's values, and what success means *to them* – not success measured by us, the organization, or anyone else. This process will serve to free the player in ways never before imagined, but most importantly, how *they* will measure success in their lives.

We have previously discussed Declarations, Intentions, and Commitments. This is a perfect tool to help move the conversation to the future or help develop new productive habits aligned with the player's values, or define their personal goals. When we get the player to state, "from now on," in essence they are making a declaration about what they intend for the future. To develop the new habit, we help the player identify behaviors and practices they will exhibit to live the declaration, or in other words, to make it intentional. After that, it is a matter of encouraging the player until these new habits take root, and the desired change comes into being.

Preparing for the Developmental Conversation

In chapter 7 we discussed the need to be present with the player. In essence this is the preparation especially needed for the Developmental Conversation. If we are present we will be available to the player; we will actively listen, we will observe, we will expose our souls, and create an environment comfortable enough for the player to expose their own soul. It is in this full presence that we muster up patience and can remain focused on someone's gifts – even when personality or other influences may make it difficult to do. And, it is in this state of full presence that we ourselves get curious, and subsequently observe the stories of our players.

The Leader Coach: Exposing Your Soul

We are firm believers that preparation for the Developmental Conversation comes by being fully present, and it is from this full presence that we make our souls available to our players. It is also in the course of conduct of these very Developmental Conversations that our risk as Leader Coaches, and as players, is at its greatest. It is for this reason that we always have to put forth our best effort, or reschedule the conversation for a later time when this best effort will be available.

In Figure 11.3 we see this presence as a corresponding relationship to the Leader Coach Evolution model, where, as we become more fully focused on the player's needs, we make our souls more available to them. In essence if we turn the pyramid over, we see that we have more emotional capacity to make ourselves available for the player. As we work our way up the pyramid into Leader Coaching the degree by which we expose our soul widens; and, the space that we have to hold others widens as well.

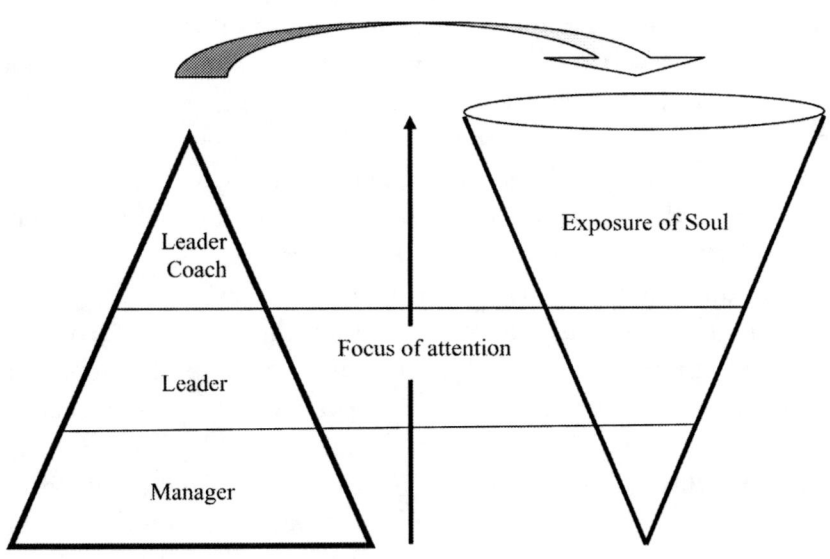

Figure 11.3

INTERFERENCE

In Tim Galwaith's book, *The Inner Game*, the author defines performance in this way:

Performance = Potential – Interference

A visual of this equation could be the clarity of the movie picture on your new high definition television. The performance is in fact the quality of the new picture. The potential is certainly equal to the technology being employed by the system for which you just shelled out big money. The interference is of course all of the negative forces such as electricity, weather, and other natural and technical disruptions.

We especially like Galwaith's model of performance, because it can be applied to all areas of our lives. What keeps us from meeting our full potential not only at work, but also with our families, communities, and relationships? Interference. The interference can be poor time management, a lack of organization, destructive habits, or a failure to understand other's needs. The majority of these behaviors stems from our emotions, and the interference our emotions pose to our behavior and desired results. The Leader Coach, through Developmental Conversations, forms an understanding of the player's emotions; and, as a result can help the player uncover the interference these emotions play in their failing to reach their full potential. After this interference is uncovered then we can help our players put practices in place to help mitigate, and ultimately remove, the interference.

The other part of this model we like is that the word *potential* is unique to each of us. Remember from Chapter 1 we defined the coach as, "The person who helps others reach more of their potential." Potential in one person may be different than that of another. Just as children produced from the same parents will often times have different abilities in school and on the athletic field, so too is it with our players. While we can strive to find the lowest common denominator for purposes of performance measurement and the management of promotions, this most assuredly does not apply when it comes to a discussion of potential.

The last thing we'll add about interference is about emotions. As we discussed in Chapter 10, it is imperative that we ensure our players are also prepared to have these conversations. In the book *Difficult*

Conversations by Stone, Patton, and Heen, they stress the need to deal with emotions before pursuing conversation. We agree that if we don't deal with the raging emotions, that there will be no listening; and, therefore, engagement in a Developmental Conversation becomes fruitless.

THE PROCESS: A HOW-TO GUIDE

We can hear our fellow coaching practitioners now, a simple linear process for coaching? Surely, the Developmental Conversation, aka the coaching conversation, is far too nuanced to be outlined in a step-by-step process. Yet, step-by-step process maps are so clean and so much easier to "hold" that we thought it would be beneficial if we could map out a common path that you could utilize in your Developmental Conversations. Please take this with a grain of salt. These conversations can be quite circular, one–step leap frogging to another or retreating back to its start. But, again, we thought it useful to have an ideal map so that you could more easily practice and understand how one step or state can lead to another. Our map of the Developmental Conversation looks something like this:

- **Presence:** We have repeated it several times, but the Developmental Conversation starts with presence. By being centered, at rest, and available to our players our soulful confidence will allow us to appreciate and love our own unique distinctions. From this fully present state, as described in chapter 7, we can set aside our own needs and insecurities and be fully available for the player. To become fully present we center our body position, we make eye contact, we lean in as an affirmation of our interest, and that we are ready to actively listen.
- **Listening:** Listening is the foundation of soulful interaction, effective coaching, and absolutely crucial to the Developmental Conversation. To let the player know we are in fact listening we parrot back what was heard, we hold eye contact, we express the emotion we hear the player feeling, and listen from their perspective, and not our own. Krisco states that when we help other's listen, it is called

coaching. We as Leader Coaches and our players need to be taught to listen not only in conversation, but also to the voices that emanate from within, and to be able to process the meaning of these inner voices. When we listen to these voices do we hear fear or joy or confusion? Our little voice or fear-based response can define how we believe others are listening. In general, listening to our inner voice serves as a great awareness tool, signaling to us that an external conversation may need to take place.

- **Agenda:** Set the agenda, and firmly grasp what the purpose of the conversation is going to be in that particular session. We may have been planning to discuss one topic, but remain flexible enough to set an alternative agenda if doing so better meets the needs of the player. The idea is to retain the flexibility, but also enough structure to preclude tangents and meandering in the scheduled conversation.
- **Observe:** Through listening, through feeling, through observation of the entire body, we see, and are fully aware of, the player's situation. We use observations of the player and ourselves to help direct the conversation and the dialogue. We help the player to self-observe through effective questioning. What do they notice? What do they feel? We acknowledge their feelings and validate our other observations. This can easily be achieved by simply checking in with the player with a simple statement and validating it's correct. For example you might share, "What I see is that when you speak of your peer, you get physically uncomfortable in your seat. Your face gets a bit red, and you seem to get a bit emotional. Is that right?" Even before sharing your observation, you may stop the conversation and ask the player what they are noticing about themselves physically; what they are feeling, and in this way help the player self-observe.
- **Curiosity:** We get curious. We don't set aside those things that come to us from listening and observing. We get curious through questioning, through observation, through wonderment. We might find the absence of feelings or

emotions interesting or, we may ask more detailed probing questions if we feel something has not been described in enough detail. Through a genuine interest in our player's well being we explore, unless the player is not ready emotionally to go there.

- **Questioning:** As we have mentioned countless times, questioning is the primary tool of the Leader Coach. Questioning in its essence is derived from curiosity and a belief in the value and inherent ability of players to address their own performance and development. Through the Socratic Method, well-considered questions guide the dialogue between Leader Coach and player. And it is in dialogue that new insights into the player's thinking, beliefs, and emotions are uncovered. How will you know what questions to ask? If you remain fully present, listen actively, and get curious the questions will come to you. The only thing to be concerned about is your intent and judgment. We are conducting an exploration, not a witch hunt. Therefore, it's important to keep your story out of the player's. What we mean by this concept is that too often we as coaches have our own stories that are driven by our thinking and belief, and we can be tempted to think that the player's story should conform to ours, which of course we think is perfectly normal and standard. Well, guess what? There is no norm or standard, so don't impose your story on the player's. The manner in which you keep judgment out of the exploration is to be careful with the words contained in your questions. There's pretty much a truth in the coaching profession that if you start your question with the word, "what," you're in safe territory. As we mentioned in Chapter 10, you should strive to eliminate the words "how" and "why" from your question, because they are words that can imply a judgment is being made. "Why did you talk to your peer in that voice?" is a loaded question. It implies, "how could you be so stupid?" So start your questions with "what," and watch your coaching skills flourish and your player's development multiply.

- **Future-based Conversation:** Move the conversation to the future, because all development lies in the future. How do we direct our dialogue to the future? By focusing on New Possibilities. To move to New Possibilities, it helps to have the player see what's going on by assisting them to become observers (as discussed above and in chapter 9). Moving their observations from "what they did" to "what they noticed" will help them bridge the conversation from the past to the future.
- **Take action:** Without action, the entire process is for naught. After we've discovered insights through questioning and envisioned different behaviors through future-based conversation, it's time to go for the gold. Through future-based conversation, we will help the player make new declarations in the form of "from now on" statements. After making these statements, we need to work with the player and put new practices in place that will help in exercising the new desired behaviors, thereby assisting the player to live their declaration. In helping the player to establish new practices we'll want to also put in place structures by which they can self-observe, and thereby self-correct their behaviors based upon that feedback. When we assist with the establishment of practices, we'll want to understand the gradient of the client, or how much change they can make at that moment, both from a developmental perspective, as well as a practicality perspective (people are busy). From the developmental perspective it's like starting a new exercise routine; start small or slowly, experience success, and gradually build up the routine. This is similar to the principle we follow when leading organizations through change. While we as the Leader Coach may have a clear picture of the end game for both our players and the organization, we will only introduce a little change at a time (remember "baby steps" from chapter 4). For if the entire change is introduced all at once we may scare people off because they may see the change as insurmountable; therefore, we introduce change a little at a time. It's like the

old adage, how do you eat an elephant; answer: one bite at a time.

THE PROCESS – AN ALTERNATIVE

Our coaching friends are correct; a Developmental Conversation is not a linear progression. A potentially better way to map out the 8-steps in the process is through the utilization of a wheel, as depicted in Figure 11.4. By visually depicting the process in this manner, each step or act in the process can be accessed from any other.

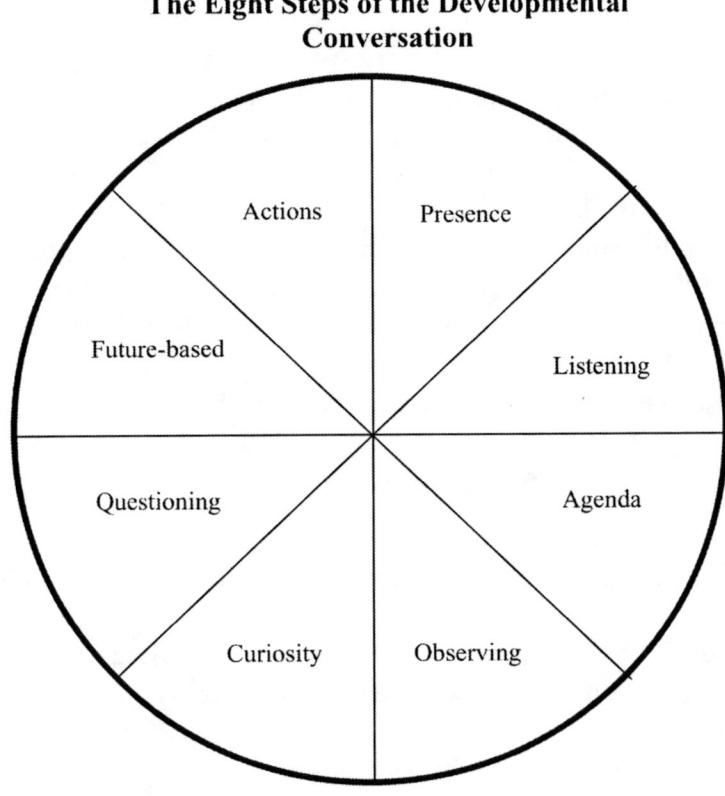

Figure 11.4

INTERNAL OBSERVATIONS OF THE COACH

We've spoken quite a bit of the need to be a keen observer of the player and to help the player to become proficient at self-observation. Yet, we should also take note of what we observe in ourselves. What do we as the coach take away from our developmental conversations? What do we observe in the player that we can apply to our own development? As we let go of our own stories and make ourselves fully present to the player, what comes back to us? Please note that the coaching and developmental process is always a two-way learning process. As we give to the player, they, and the coaching process, give back to us.

The last note on observation is the need to observe the player's emotions/feelings and body. All too often in the developmental process we get "stuck in the head," or "in the mind." When we get stuck in the mind, we and our players try to *think* our way through an issue and its accompanying process, quite often shutting off our emotions and not considering the value of the feedback from these emotions and feelings. The body too is a great signaling device. If we become aware and help our players become aware of the body's reaction to stress, fear, and happiness, we can then use the body as one more observation tool. Our bodies can be early warning devices of emotions. Through constant observation, we can equate certain feelings in the body with certain emotional reactions. And then, over time, we will learn to align emotional reactions with required corrective feedback.

ASSESSING THE ENVIRONMENT

Coaches need to assess the mood of the organization or environment in which the player plays or functions. This is one of the benefits the Leader Coach has over the Executive Coach. Because of his own position within the organization, the Leader Coach should have a *full* appreciation of the environment and the impact it may be having on the player. Of course this is a double-edged sword, in that, the Leader Coach may either be so engulfed in the environment, or may be part of the environmental difficulty itself. Ideally, the Leader Coach will be in a position to respect the situation in which the player is surrounded, and help provide different possibilities for them regarding both their story about the mood and environment, as well as expand the possibilities available to them in the prevailing mood or environment. Most likely, the player has created a story or will be living in a prevailing organizational story built upon folklore assessments of facts. The Leader Coach can help to shift the mood of the organization by sharing a different story and perspective about the facts.

THE CONTINUAL NEED FOR RECOVERY

A benefit of the Developmental Conversation is that it should help the player (and us) define our values. One of the greatest reasons for understanding our core values is to aid us in the development of a mechanism by which we can deal with fear when it rears it's ugly head. For no matter how confident and well grounded we are, fear *will* make cameo appearances to all of us. As we spoke of earlier in the book, fear can impact us in a wide variety of ways. For purposes of this current discussion, it has a tendency to force a player (and we are all players ourselves) off center or off track. Without a firm understanding of who we are at our core, it is difficult to recover from this fear when it appears. For if we are attempting to recover, or re-center ourselves, from a fear response, if we have not identified the essence of who and what we are, to what inner personality will we recover? In the Developmental Conversation it will be not only incumbent upon the coach to help the player identify his set of fears and the persona within when we are behaving from a state of fear, but we will also want to assist the player identify and get comfortable with the essence of themselves: their soul.

In this manner, we help the player create more choices for themselves by developing increased self-awareness. This matured self awareness and ability to recover allows the player to have greater opportunity to live their Intention.

FINAL THOUGHTS

Some final thoughts before we close this chapter. First, to be a coach we must be coached. To be effective to our players, we need to continue to develop new insights within our own development. This growth enables us to perceive it in those around us. The only way to achieve this is by being coached and being in a constant state of development ourselves. Being coached keeps us grounded, and provides a practice for continued development.

We mentioned it earlier, but this is definitely not intended to be a one-way street. We as Leader Coaches will receive just as much as we give. As we nourish and enrich our souls, our souls grow, and our souls are developed. When this growth occurs, we in turn help our players feed *their* souls. Why do we make the choice to be Leader Coaches? For most of us, it is because it feeds our calling or desire to serve others; but, we also do it for ourselves. It is also about us living in the manner that Whitworth advocates, and making it all about people living fully, passionately, enjoying their work and giving their best effort. Fulfillment is not something that will happen someday when you're rich or famous, but is available this moment and the next for those on a path of fulfillment. We as Leader Coaches endeavor to hike this path of fulfillment as often as possible and we seek to have others join us for the journey.

In one of the author's early journals, he uncovered this entry defining the Leader Coach: "The Leader Coach helps others find purpose and align their skills, professional, and role with that purpose. It is a way for people to find what their life's work is all about, holding their work out as something noble, and a way to live it with their uniqueness. It really is all about loving oneself and others by defining one's self-purpose and overcoming the demons of one's past to live that purpose fully."

Conclusion

Conversation is the tool used to convey your love, which we believe to be the absolute key to effective leadership. It begins with loving yourself, and being completely comfortable with your own character, values, and in turn being authentic with your message and mission. It continues by loving your purpose in life, and finding that it is truly noble and worth following. Finally, as a leader it means truly loving your followers, and compelling them to devote themselves to their own development, and in turn to love themselves. This innate self confidence and acceptance fosters love of their peers, and leaders, and a compelling desire to want to follow the inspired vision that you have shared as a leader.

PART V

*Enhancements:
Exponential Gifts of the Leader Coach*

By definition, an enhancement is something that improves or makes greater. In this final section we are going to examine the three attributes of *Energy, Ownership,* and *Giving* which we believe are three additional keys to the successful relationship between the Leader Coach and player.

In Energy, we will share some thoughts about how it is incumbent upon the Leader Coach to instill energy into the players both individually and as a group. We can achieve this by being visible and accessible, by being real, and bringing passion, fun, and likewise making it real for the team. We also make it happen by being a source of energy to our team.

In Ownership, we address the questions of who owns the process, and the relationship, and to whom we should dedicate our efforts and provide coaching. We will also determine that we can't want success for our players more than they want it for themselves! We will also attempt to discern some rule of thumb on when we must sever the relationship and to 'pull the plug' because of a lack of commitment on the part of the player.

In Giving, it is about escaping the Ivory Tower, and being a true field leader. Mixing it up with the players, and being a hands-on leader which is most certainly a great distinction from the role of Manager or Coach.

Finally, we'll put a bow on the whole package by wrapping up with some conclusions drawn from each of the chapters. We believe that Coaching is the greatest gift that we can receive and share with the members of our team.

Chapter 12

Energy

The very mention of the word *energy* conjures up many different images. Some see it as power generated by huge turbines such as those at Hoover Dam, others see it as the exuberance of a child, or the manner in which said child can play and play all day long seemingly like the energizer bunny. Others use it as a word of admiration, and refer to it as the ability of an individual to complete endless tasks, or to inspire those around them.

Following on that description, *energy* would be simply the ability to do *work*. While work (or output) is often measured in the same terms as energy, we want to distinguish between these two forces. Likewise, we want to define and distinguish energy as being different than *power* and *force*. In terms of physics, a subject we avoided in high school, preferring girls instead, *force* is a push or a pull on an object or body. The amount of work is determined by the strength of the force used and the distance through which it moves. Power measures the rate at which work is done. Sound like a circuitous argument? Yeah, we agree, thus reaffirming our choice of high school electives.

We could muddy the water some more, and mention that man has found ways to release energy to do work, such as when they change energy of a waterfall into electrical energy, which they can further change into power for electrical appliances. We can use heat to boil water and convert it into steam, which will power a steam engine, and in turn propel a locomotive.

Staying with the physics environ for just another paragraph or two, the law related to the conservation of energy states that the amount of energy in the universe is always the same. It can be neither increased nor decreased. You can only get as much energy or force out of any given machine in direct proportion to that which is put into it. This is called efficiency. To derive the efficiency rating, we simply take the amount of energy we get out of a machine divided by the amount of energy put into the machine. So, if a machine returns one-half of the energy that is being put in, it has a rating of 50% efficiency. You hear about your furnace as having a *high energy efficiency rating*. Don remembers replacing his old furnace that possessed a 60% efficiency rating, which meant that it was delivering only 96,000 BTUs of heat from a 160,000 BTU power plant. Not very good, especially in cold Chicago winters. When replaced with a newfangled high efficiency furnace with a rating of 93%, the 132,000 BTU power plant was actually providing 122,760 units of warmth! Less energy going in, and yet a greater return, or *efficiency* in return. Nuclear powered equipment such as submarines and aircraft carriers have a very high efficiency rating, being able to go to sea without refueling for up to twenty years!

Interestingly enough, human beings have a very low mechanical efficiency rating of about 24%. The efficiency rating on an unemployed brother-in-law, who may be living with you, may be even lower.

Sometimes the energy flow is modified however. By this we mean that the form of the output may be different than that of the input. For example, most electrical energy going into an electrical motor comes out in a revised form of energy usually mechanical, and will be utilized to turn shafts that will either pump, drill, or cause some other activity to occur. The total energy in and out is the same, but the form is different.

So what does this physics lesson on energy have to do with the subject of leadership generally, and coaching specifically? Actually, it is a very accurate analogy. One only has to pause and think about the leaders for whom we have worked, or served under, or reported to, and very quickly we can distinguish between those we enjoyed and those we did not enjoy. We can certainly also draw a correlation to the amount of *energy* that these leaders either did, or did not, bring to their role. We can also consider whether they shared with us either directly in the form of oral and written encouragement, or through words and deeds that served to inspire a shared vision, the passion with which he or she approached all of their own duties.

We can also consider developing an efficiency rating for our leaders in the same manner as our physics example. How much energy does our team produce as a percentage of the energy investment on the part of the leader? How can we improve on this rating? By looking within our own souls at the brand of inspiration that we are providing to our teams, and determining whether we are instilling in our teams a desire to achieve more and to follow their leader.

ETERNAL FLAME

We believe that it is incumbent upon the Leader Coach to instill the energy into the group. Not all of it, and certainly not all of the time, but needs to remain a constant and ready source, much like the eternal flame. This is critical especially under difficult and trying conditions. One of the greatest examples of this was the manner in which Mayor Rudy Giuliani demonstrated incredible leadership in the aftermath of the World Trade Center attacks on September 11, 2001.

TIME Magazine in selecting Mayor Giuliani as the Person of the Year, cited: "[f]or having more faith in us than we had in ourselves, for being brave when required and rude where appropriate and tender without being trite, for not sleeping and not quitting and not shrinking from the pain all around him, Rudy Giuliani, Mayor of the World, is *TIME* 2001 Person of the Year."

Television news coverage of the horrifying events that day and the days that followed seemingly had Mayor Giuliani everywhere. From the devastation located at Ground Zero, and the City's Emergency Management Center, to the sites of various and sundry funerals as well as makeshift shelters, and the City's family support center. Through his unflagging desire to *be there* for the people of *his* city, Rudy Giuliani showed true leadership by being the very nucleus of the recovery and relief efforts that followed. In addition to being *visible*, he remained *accessible*, to those who needed their elected leader. It must also be said that through his energy, Rudy Giuliani was able to bring people together in a true non-partisan effort, and to draw on the great resources of companies such as General Electric, Home Depot, Dell, AOL,

WorldCom, as millions of dollars of equipment, supplies, and cash donations flowed feely. A heinous and senseless act of terrorism had not defeated the spirit of either the city or the country, but rather forced the release of hidden or newly found reserves of energy, patriotism, and compassion. It began with an Army of One, and the energy of Rudy Guiliani.

BEING REAL

As we have already discussed, Trust is the number one attribute that followers look for in their leaders. The attribute of trust is seemingly a manifestation of a leader's character, which in turn is derived from a leader's instilled values. It is a leader's character that conveys to the follower a sense of predictability on the part of the leader, which in turn prompts comfort and reassurance in his followers.

The art of being real is more than predictability or consistency. It is about being an energy source; an energy source of optimism, hope, and confidence. Relating back to what a leader is, and how it is important for him to *Be, Know,* and *Do* those things on a reliable basis, by being present, and being real. A leader has both the ability and the duty to interact with his followers, his peers, and his superiors, breeding energy and goodwill. This energy is exponentially returned by those around him, further confirming that a leader's influence has the ability to initiate and sustain change.

FORMS OF ENERGY

Both authors in the course of their journey through Fortune 200 companies have been exposed to countless reorganizations and changes in corporate direction. Most of these wholesale changes were accompanied by the infusion of marketing campaigns with accompanying buttons, flyers, posters, DVDs, satellite broadcasts, commercials, news print, and often contests, promotions, and other incentives. These positive *external* infusions of energy often have a very limited shelf life, and when the confetti has fallen, and the balloons have lost their air, like a flickering candle, the energy can wane, and finally go out. So what happens then?

In organizations that have strong, energetic leaders, these programs can survive, and even prosper, because of the *internal* energy of these leaders. It is the constant energy flow of these leaders that make long term change both plausible and possible.

Another analogy of the distinctive difference between the lasting effects of external and internal energy would be the difference between throwing balls of wadded up paper on a campfire as opposed to building the fire up to the point where a larger, slow burning log can be added to the fire. The paper readily ignites, is deceptively bright, burns tall, but throws off very little heat. The log on the other hand, is enduring; it burns hot; and provides, in addition to the aforementioned light, a source of real, sustainable heat for both cooking and survival. The glowing embers of the log are analogous to the glow of the leader's energy flow. Followers look to their leader for the warmth and life saving effects of this energy and fire. It is this fire that allows the leader to inspire a shared vision. Not artificial or superficial like the paper, no spin, no plastic, but a very real source of confidence and enthusiasm that precedes the attainment of mission accomplishment.

Combat Energy

We have recounted for you the heroic battlefield exploits of Audie Murphy (*To Hell and Back*) and Dick Winters (*Band of Brothers*), in terms of inspiring battlefield courage and mission accomplishment. Even more than courage, guidance, and direction, troops look to their leaders, especially under these arduous conditions, to provide them with a certain level of safety, but more than anything else, to provide them with much needed energy. Don's own troop leading experiences confirm that successful lieutenants, captains, and field grade officers never are tired. It just is not part of the scenario. They are the ones trooping the line in the middle of the night insuring that troops are alert, or leading the convoys of vehicles, and in turn rallying sagging energy reserves in order that mission requirements can be achieved. Seventy two hours without sleep of any kind is not unusual. When pushed, the human body can deliver additional adrenalin reserves for ninety six and even one hundred twenty hours.

A classic historical example of how a leader's energy can extract the seemingly impossible from his troops would be General George Patton's one hundred mile dash with elements of the Third Army to relieve the Screaming Eagles of the 101st Airborne in Bastogne at the outset of the Battle of the Bulge. What did Third Army do in the snow covered countryside in the days before Christmas, 1944? They disengaged from one battle, pivoted, force marched one hundred miles, and then re-engaged the enemy without rest, little in supply and equipment replenishment, and only a desire to save their brothers in arms from annihilation. What made it possible? Most certainly it was the vision and energy of a commander who was willing to endure the rigors and hardships of his men, and to lead from the front, but more importantly by sharing his seemingly infinite well of energy.

True North

So are you getting the idea that a Leader does more than provide direction and inspiration to his followers? We cannot stress strongly enough how important it is for the Leader, particularly the Leader Coach to always be present, to remain calm and unruffled, even in the face of overwhelming odds, for it most assuredly is up to him to set the tone, and to remain the constant True North from which everyone takes their lead.

Followers, particularly younger ones new to the organization, who have greater needs in the way of reassurance and reaffirmation, need the constancy of their leaders, and will look to them to remain on an even keel, and to be the port in which any storm can be weathered.

Energy as Enthusiasm

Vince Lombardi, the legendary coach of the NFL's Green Bay Packers, often spoke of passion and enthusiasm as being the seeds of success. People who knew Lombardi said that he embraced life to its fullest, and approached the things that he loved with the zeal of a missionary. This zeal is something that can't be hidden, and is most assuredly contagious to those around us. This is the raw energy that we are talking about that leaders possess. Like a pilot light on a furnace or hot water heater, the Leader's energy is always there. At times it is low key and resonates with a quiet hum such as that of a nuclear reactor.

Quiet, sleek, but incredibly powerful. Other times it is loud and brash like the energy being released from a thunder and lightning storm. Leaders and their enthusiasm can be the difference between success and defeat. At the Battle of Gettysburg, the timid, lackluster leadership on the part of General Robert E. Lee's Corps commanders, made the outcome of the battle a victory for the North, just as the failure to pursue and destroy Lee's army in its retreat, prolonged the war. A lack of energy on the part of the leaders of both armies is a glaring example of how the absence of energy will deny the follower both the vision and desire to continue the fight.

Positive Energy

A coach's positive energy can instill the will to win in his players, and its absence can most assuredly doom a team to defeat. Rick Pitino, head coach of the University of Kentucky Wildcats, learned that the manner in which he approached potential game winning time outs had a profound impact on his players. When he applied pressure, rather than providing encouragement, these sessions became the precursor to self-fulfilling prophesies in which the team would not execute, and the game would be lost. By changing his own mindset, and by instituting an aggressive pre-game program based on positive energy being generated from a foundation of extensive practice sessions, wargaming, and getting to know his players on a one on one basis, Pitino altered the team's overall energy structure. By implanting the belief that victory is a natural offshoot of their practice, and that their confidence is deserved, this positive energy has produced success and national championships.

More than simply just viewing the glass half-full rather than half-empty, Pitino has raised winning and the infusion of positive energy into his team to an art form, and has reduced it down to a matter of choice. His players can choose their attitude when they get out of bed, striving for the positive, and then being enriched by the positive energy of their coach. As the title of his book clearly indicates, *Success is a Choice*. A coach's positive energy has the ability to be the catalyst that catapults a team from mediocrity to greatness.

Conclusion

A leader truly is the nucleus of the team he leads when it comes to the infusion of energy, power, and focus. Rudy Giuliani personified this in the aftermath of September 11th for the City of New York, and the World as it watched in horror and then admiration. Through his unflagging desire to *be there* for the people of *his* city, Rudy Giuliani showed true leadership by being the very nucleus of the recovery and relief efforts that followed. In addition to being *visible,* he remained *accessible,* to those who needed their elected leader to supply them with hope, vision, reassurance, and renewed energy.

Chapter 13

Ownership

Ownership by definition is simply the state of being an owner. An owner is subsequently defined as a person who owns. Following in this line, and hopefully a little more insightful and relevant to this discussion, to own means to have or to possess, or to acknowledge or to belong to oneself. It is this latter portion of the definition that we believe to be the most relevant for purposes of discussion as to whom actually owns the coaching relationship.

Who Owns the Relationship?

We believe that the relationship between the Leader Coach and his player has to be mutually owned by both of them. As the Leader Coach, we have a deep and abiding responsibility for the relationship because of the inherent power and authority that we bring to the relationship. We must remain on guard so as not to ever abuse the authority of our office, or to impose our will. This being said, we also have the reciprocal responsibility of maintaining the propriety of the relationship, and to insure that we don't allow the player to take advantage of the relationship. As the Leader Coach we also have the responsibility of representing the simultaneous, mutual, and diverse interests of both the player and the organization that we serve. Our ultimate goal as a Leader Coach should be to influence outcomes and inspire others by demonstrating our own congruence, the attributes of character that we possess, as well as the intestinal fortitude to stay the course and to take the initiative in the areas of challenging the process and empowering others to act.

The first rule in establishing the relationship is to let the player set the agenda. By this we mean that the Player should be empowered to define the overall objectives of the coaching relationship to be achieved, whereas the Leader Coach is permitted to assist in framing up the objectives as well as the schedule by which they will be achieved and implemented. It is imperative that the Leader Coach be willing to relinquish control to the Player at this phase of the relationship.

Ultimately, based on the stated objectives as framed up by the player, the Leader Coach will have to make a determination as to whether he accepts the goals, buys into the agreement, and can be effective in coaching the player. If there is any concern about the viability of the relationship, the Leader Coach should not agree to step into a coaching role, and should remain in the role of leader to the player.

Who Gets the Coaching?

Many years ago, in a galaxy far far away, it used to be that there was a negative stigma attached to being a player who was being coached. Companies spent tens of thousands of dollars on players that were at best marginal for "get well" programs. Players did not want to be coached because it was a sign that they were not measuring up, and could face a less than desired career path. Then one day, a wise Chief Executive Officer hit upon the idea that maybe it would make sense to spend this money on rising stars, or executives with a clearly defined career path in front of them. Thus, executive coaching became an award, or badge of honor that was sought after by these rising stars, and coaching was good. So, share your coaching skills with your stars and see their energy rise, and the results of your team flourish.

We Can't Want it More than They Do!

A key to remember as you enter into the coaching relationship is that we cannot want this relationship, or the accompanying success we hope to bring to bear, more than the player himself wants it. Just as a little league coach cannot will a youngster to perfect his swing or to throw a faster fast ball, or a curve ball that breaks more, so too here.

The desire to achieve has to be evident inside the player's character, and demonstrated by his willingness to work at the relationship, to internalize the coaching that results, and to then apply it. We cannot will a person to be more successful. In other words, as a Leader Coach, it is neither possible or proper for us to impose our will on them, nor should we allow them to drag us down or hold us back in the event that they determine that they don't have the heart to pursue the mutually reached goals.

If this occurs, then both the Player and the Leader Coach fail in their assigned roles. An example of where this could happen is the same little league scenario. In concept, little league exists to expose young children to the fundamentals of baseball, sportsmanship, and teamwork. What has happened over the years in a great many of the little league programs around the country is that over zealous adults have mutated the program by placing the children under pressure to perform, and eliminated the fun aspect of it all. In essence, the adults were living vicariously through their kids, wanting to play the game more than them.

Another pitfall to avoid is the temptation of providing too much leadership, or slipping into a role that more resembles that of mentor, where our subject matter expertise may become more prominent, or we become the little league coach who rather than instilling a love for the game in these young people, in turn frustrates, and potentially even hurts them as players.

How Do We Know Whom To Invest Our Time?

This is perhaps one of the more difficult questions that a Leader Coach must ask himself. Since we cannot possibly give everyone all of the attention that they may want or warrant, or simply that we wish to impart to them, how do we prioritize in whom we invest our time? Some would have us believe that we should only invest our time in the "A" players of our organization, or namely those people who potentially will provide us and the organization with the greatest return. Simply put, if you remember our lessons on energy and efficiency measurement from the previous chapter, the premise here would be that an investment in these players is like providing more energy to a higher efficient machine, which will in turn generate more output. It follows then that this school of thought would also discourage us from spending anything more than a minimal amount of time with the "B" and "C" players. The authors have heard these "C" players inappropriately referred to as "bottom feeders" and other derogatory terms by their "A" player counterparts.

An opposing school of thought would be that the typical "A" player is more self sufficient, and therefore less inclined to *need* or *want* our attention, and therefore it is proper for us to work with the lesser players, with the intent of transforming the "B" player of promise into an "A" player, and to raise the "C" player to an acceptable level in the "B" range.

We do not subscribe to either school of thought, and recognize that quite often that the Leader Coach will be in a position whereby he will have to conduct assessments of his team members, and determine for himself what the proper mix of support and coaching will be to his team members. An illustration of this time-based recipe can be found in Figure 11.2. For this reason, we view both leadership and coaching as an art form, and not an exact science. The important thing to remember is that the coach's primary responsibility is to provide nurturing support to the player in such a manner so as to assist the player in the Socratic Method so that they in turn discover answers to their own issues.

SO WHEN DO WE PULL THE PLUG?

The manner in which a Leader needs to approach the role of Leader Coach, and sometimes know when to "pull the plug" can be depicted in a simple illustration. Many years ago, one of the authors was responsible for the physical conditioning of the troops assigned to his military unit. One element of the Army's physical fitness test was a timed, two-mile run. Contrary to what one sees in the movies, not everyone who goes into the military can run, most certainly not in the perfectly choreographed formations where everyone sings along effortlessly. This limitation on running does not distinguish between age, rank, or assignment. Simply put, some people are just not runners. Unfortunately, that was *not* one of the options available if one was in the Army. The author's dubious job was to make those who were struggling into enough of a runner so as to successfully negotiate the physical fitness test.

The author learned that the best way to encourage a person to run is not to stand on the sidelines and to use a bull horn, or to threaten them with negative consequences such as adverse efficiency ratings, remedial training, or even potential discharge, but rather to do it the old fashioned way, and simply to run along side of them. Running, sweating, encouraging them, and helping them to develop additional stamina by insuring that they did not start to walk, but continued to run, and slowly, over time, to increase the pace, and to ultimately train them to the appropriate standard.

As a coach, the author was willing to do this as often, and for as long, as necessary so long as the player continued to run. Whining and puking aside, when the player either ceased to demonstrate the appropriate level of commitment and dedication, or *began to walk*, the author would leave this individual and move on to the next person who required coaching. Was this an overly simplistic approach to coaching these individuals? Was it Darwinism at its worst? Absolutely. However, the coach was selflessly serving the player, encouraging the heart, and modeling the way, and was willing to continue the relationship *for as long as the player put forth the requisite effort*. When the player stopped, so did the relationship. The end result was that those players who either asked for, or accepted, the obviously needed coaching, were successful. This required them to put forth the requisite effort, and to remain steadfast in their determination to achieve applicable fitness standards. Was it easy? No. But success was achieved because of the relationship of trust that existed between coach and player. It is important to note that during these coaching sessions, that the author was coaching not only enlisted subordinates, but also several superior officers. Yeah, that was fun. Not.

A Final Note About Running

We have mentioned in previous chapters the importance of the Leader Coach sharing the hardships of his players, while appearing to be above them, as in the example of not sweating in the desert, as well as the necessity of having the requisite character traits that inspired confidence in the players. Going back to the same military running example, Don found that the very best way to inspire the troops was to be in the best shape that he could be in, and when possible, to be the very best.

Immediately after Vietnam, the standard for attaining one hundred points on the two-mile run was to be able to run it in 11:09. This was the standard for the youngest age bracket. It should be noted that the older a soldier gets, the more time he or she is allocated for completing this run. We guess the enemy should be clued into these standards so that they will only shoot at the younger faster soldiers. In any event, Don was pretty proud of the fact that he could consistently run the two miles in less than 10:39, even on occasion breaking the 10:00 barrier. As one of the lieutenants in the battery, that was a good thing. The only thing that made it less than perfect was a man by the name of Jack Rabbit Bergeron, who would *always* do it in less than ten minutes. This naturally sparked some good natured competition, but as a [young] leader, Don must candidly admit to the frustration associated with eating this guy's dust nearly every time we ran as a unit. Nonetheless, he was grateful that between them, they could inspire a few more to aspire to the 11:09 mark. This presented numerous opportunities for coaching to an enhanced performance standard that would not otherwise have been present.

An Example About Being Out Front and On the Phones

Okay, time to check the military testosterone levels, and to relate this chapter back to an organization that you are more likely to be a part. As we have mentioned on several occasions, it is important for the leader, and particularly the Leader Coach, to walk the walk as well as simply to talk the talk. This is especially important in a sales organization, where you are only as good as your last sale.

One of the authors was up in Boston on one of his weekly sojourns from Richmond, VA, and two of the sales managers had arranged for the author to conduct a phone clinic for the sales agents. The clinic went very well, with great participation and interaction by the agents, and then the time came for them to get on the phones and to actually call potential clients to set appointments. One particularly brave agent asked if he might "observe the maestro on the phones." After addressing a bit of irrational fear, based mainly on the potential for embarrassment, or *failing* to be as effective as when an agent himself, he swallowed hard and took a deep breath. Phone numbers were produced, and the Divisional

Vice President got on the phones, to discover that it was just like riding a bike. The ability to model the way, or in this case, picking up the telephone and setting appointments by demonstrating an acquired technical competence, enhanced all future coaching in the two regions going forward. Nothing says it better than modeling the way and just doing it. Being there, making phone calls side by side, letting them *see* a manner in which to do it, rather than being *told* how to do it as with mentoring, not only raised morale, but increased productivity on an exponential basis. It also presented a great opportunity for true coaching to continue in the months ahead. The players had most notably set the standards and expectations for this coaching session and had benefited from the session, as did the coach.

Conclusion

The relationship between Leader Coach and player is unique. To be successful, it must be based on a foundation of mutual respect and trust. The Leader Coach and player enter into a contract based on commitment towards the enhanced performance and/or development of a specific skill set on the part of the player. It requires commitment on the part of both the Leader Coach and the player. Neither one is allowed to breach any of the terms of the contract without damaging and potentially ending the relationship.

The player should be empowered to define the overall objectives of the coaching relationship to be achieved, whereas the Leader Coach is permitted to assist in framing up the objectives, as well as the schedule by which they will be achieved and implemented. It is imperative that the Leader Coach be willing to relinquish control to the Player at this phase of the relationship. It is in essence a contract between the Leader Coach and the player, and *not* simply a leader's demand.

When properly executed, this coaching relationship inspires growth and enhanced performance on the part of both participants and leaves a legacy upon which future relationships and multi-generations of coaching relationships can exist.

As the Leader Coach we also have the responsibility of representing the simultaneous, mutual, and diverse interests of both the player and the organization that we serve. Our ultimate goal as a Leader Coach should be to influence outcomes and inspire others by demonstrating our own congruence, the attributes of character that we possess, as well as the intestinal fortitude to stay the course and to take the initiative in the areas of challenging the process and empowering others to act.

We cannot will a person to be more successful. In other words, as Leader Coaches, it is neither possible or proper for us to impose our will on them, nor should we allow them to drag us down or hold us back in the event that they determine that they don't have the heart to pursue the mutually reached goals.

Chapter 14

Giving

If you thought being a Leader Coach was something that you can simply do on company time, without any real investment on your part, forget it. Or that it would prove to be an easy task, free from peril and risk, simply because you are approaching the relationship from the vantage point of boss, or superior, well, surprise, this is not the case at all. As we mentioned in previous chapters, it does not matter whether the player you are coaching is a valued employee, a rising superstar, or even your own child, there is *always* an inherent element of risk present. If for no other reason than as a coach you always have an emotional investment in the relationship primarily because you will always be in the role of giver.

Calvin Coolidge, President of the United States in the early 20th Century was known as "Silent Cal." He earned this moniker by simply not saying a lot of anything, to include the six years that he was our country's Chief Executive. However, one very noteworthy comment that is attributed to him is "no person was ever honored for what he received. Honor has been the reward for what he gave." We believe that this very succinctly makes the point of what being a Leader Coach is really all about: giving.

We've mentioned that as leaders we leave our fingerprints on those whom we lead – it can either be in a positive or negative manner – we can either lift up, or push down, all the while living vicariously through these people and their achievements. Well, the way we put this into action is to escape the ivory tower, and to lead from in front of the desk – not behind it. It means that we have to stay in touch with the world around us, and as mentioned in the previous chapter on Ownership, be willing to step out of our comfort zone, and to take a little risk by flirting with failure of the relationship. Nothing says it better than when we reach down deep inside, and give a bit of ourselves, and expose our heart and soul.

If you recall, we have put forth the proposition that a good coach is one that is also being coached and personally growing all the while he is coaching others. This means passing on, or passing down, what we learn in the course of our own journey, to the people who really need it. We can only accomplish this by being engaged, and firmly in the game. We can't coach from the sidelines. It means getting out from behind the security and safety of our desks and offices, and getting out to the field, or on to the floor of the factory, or in front of the group, by being visible and accessible, and truly exposing our souls.

We said way back in the Preface that leaders come in all shapes and sizes, male, female, young, old; some are managers, some are organizers, some are control freaks or simply doers, conversely, some are coated in Teflon because nothing sticks to them, and they even find a way to delegate responsibility, and in rare cases, even authority. Some are mentors, and some are great leaders because they inspire others to act simply through the influence of their words and example. But for one of these leaders to become a Leader Coach, and to take the leap to the top of the pyramid as depicted in chapter 2, a Leader Coach must be willing to give of himself.

Giving, by definition, means to give. Yes, we know, another insightful 'duh,' insofar as definitions go. Amazingly enough however, the simple word *give* takes up a full half page of the World Book dictionary. It was interesting to view all of the various manners in which it can be used as either a transitive or intransitive verb. The definitions ranged from "to hand over as a present without pay," to "hand over in return for something," "to let have," "to offer or present," "to furnish or supply," "to dedicate or devote," or "to sacrifice, relinquish, or surrender." The list goes on and on. For purposes of this illustration, we believe that what a Leader Coach *gives* to his player is a piece of himself, his heart, and his soul. It reflects a desire on the part of the coach to impart acquired wisdom, insight, the very essence of his character, and, all of this is given away *gratis*, or at no cost to the player. At times, it may even represent a sacrifice on the part of the coach, but for the most part, it is something that we freely relinquish for the betterment of the player individually, and the team as a whole. This being said, keep in mind that our expectation is that the coach too will be the recipient of something back from the player(s) as well as from the ongoing relationship with his own coach.

It would also appear obvious that associated with every facet of giving is the act of selflessness. However, before delving too deeply into this aspect of giving, we want to qualify it. In his book *The Giving Tree*, a tale of a giant tree and a young boy who advances through the various stages of life until he is finally an old man, author Shel Silverstein illustrates giving until there is nothing left to give. A beautifully crafted story, that is simultaneously thought provoking and a heart touching illustration of total dedication, we also believe that it is more appropriately reserved for a relationship such as that of parent and child, which is probably the ultimate Leader Coach-Player relationship. For purposes of our discussion, this is well beyond the level of giving that we would expect to find in a relationship between Leader Coach and player.

Another aspect of the giving relationship involves the level of commitment on the part of the coach and the player. Another light but effective analogy of which we are fond, deals with the word *commitment*. By definition, commitment means a pledge or promise. It is clear that when it comes to the chicken and the pig, it would be fair that both are committed to providing us humans with our daily breakfast. The chicken shows her commitment by providing the eggs for our breakfast table. Day in and day out, we are treated to these white and yellow gems of the barnyard, consuming millions of them boiled, fried, scrambled, poached, and any other manner in which we desire. Even if the chicken is only half-heartedly committed to the process, we continue to eat. The pig on the other hand, has only one shot at glory, and therefore must be *really* committed to our breakfast table if they are to provide the bacon. Both of these examples are far more extreme than what we are advocating for level of commitment between the coach and the player, as well as their level of giving.

For this reason, both the coach and the player have to remain aware of just how much the coach *is* giving to the player. Like the chicken, it is okay if through the various Social, Performance, and Developmental Conversations, the coach is providing the eggs for the player's breakfast table. Ideally, the player is likewise enriching the coach by providing feedback and insights that allow the coach to feel self-actualization. What both have to be wary of is when the player determines that he craves something *more* than just eggs. Both must guard against the time that either consciously or sub-consciously, the player wants a drumstick or another piece of meat. While we have maintained that the art of coaching requires selflessness, it most assuredly does not require self sacrifice.

So how do we, as a Leader Coach, give to our players, in a manner that reflects the requisite selflessness, without it becoming completely one-sided and draining to the coach? By setting, marking, and maintaining very distinct boundaries from the time that the coaching contract is established, and the relationship commences between the parties.

WHAT DOES A LEADER COACH *REALLY* GIVE?

A Leader Coach, more than anything else, is a provider of hope. He provides the players on his team with encouragement, and gets people excited. A Leader Coach also provides influence and direction by setting the example to those around him.

A Leader Coach lifts up those around him by sharing praise freely but sincerely, and by providing inspiration and vision. A Leader Coach must be as quick, if not quicker, to recognize good work as they are bad work. A Leader Coach gives knowledge and skills to their players by both modeling the way and by sharing the larger perspective, or big picture, and by drawing out the natural skills and talents of the player by asking Socratic questions, rather than resorting to simple mentoring.

Another gift from the coach to the player is loyalty. While this is something that can be given far more freely and readily by a coach to a player simply as a matter of choice, the converse is not true. For the loyalty of subordinates must be earned by the coach, through his words, his actions, and most certainly, his character.

Something that one of the authors learned while serving as a senior sales leader was the axiom of "the more leadership you give away, the more you get back in return." This sometimes requires us to go outside our own comfort zone, and to display more than a little bit of faith in both the act as well as our subordinates. Sometimes it is a flat out challenge to the paradigms by which we ourselves operate! However, we can greatly strengthen our relationships and advance our mutual causes by allowing our subordinates to spread their wings. We have to trust our players, and show them that we trust them through applying this axiom. By using our own authority to empower others, we ultimately strengthen the chain of leadership that we are building within our organization. If we as the leader, retain this authority, there is no energy being infused into our relationships or the lives of our players.

Finally, a coach always gives love, and is generous. As we heard from Coach Vince Lombardi back in chapter 5, love has a very large and very real place in every organization. You may not always like your players, but as the coach, you must love them. This can often be a real stumbling block for the leader who is struggling with becoming a Leader Coach.

Coach Lou Holtz advanced the thought that when you love people, you don't just blindly give them whatever they think they need or want, but rather you help them identify all of their options, and lead them to making the best choice for themselves. Make it real for them by personalizing it, and get the player to have some skin in the game. The example he used was the wedding he was willing to pay for when his daughter chose to wed. He told her that he would give her as nice a wedding as she wanted, and the planning continued to progress, and the price tag rose and rose. Finally, he said that he would pay up to a certain level. He also proposed that if the arrangements were scaled back, that he would write a check to the bride and groom for the difference between the actual cost and the ceiling that he had established. Nearly immediately, the two bands became one, and thought was even given to utilizing the services of a DJ. As soon as the money became *real* to the bride and groom, so did their expectations and desires. Ultimately, the check that Coach Holtz wrote was enough to help the young couple with a down payment on their first home. Through his willingness to give, he gave an even greater gift: choice.

Another of our favorite authors, John Maxwell, in his work, *The 21 Irrefutable Laws of Leadership*, refers to the Law of Legacy. The Law of Legacy as Maxwell explains it is the leader's ability to determine the law of succession behind him. To this end, he observes that it is critical, for any organization that desires to grow and prosper, to make developing a new generation of leaders a part of the culture, and that regardless of how strong a leader is, he cannot go it alone. Whether it is Phil Jackson or Lou Holtz or Joe Torre, at the helm of the team, he would be nothing without a team of good players to lead. One of the greatest gifts a leader can give to his players as well as the organization is the ability to succeed with an ever increasing line of leadership and bench strength.

APPLYING THE LAW OF LEGACY

How do we know that we have been successful as a leader, and given the gift of leadership to our players and followers? One rule that Don has applied for a great many years, is that it is important to leave 'it' better than when you found it. Whether it is command of a military unit, or leadership of a sales organization, or an auxiliary at church, the goal should always be to leave it in better condition than when you found it.

While this may sound simplistic, it has proven to be an easy method in discerning whether and when, your work is done, and the time is right to move on to the next challenge and opportunity.

An added gift to the organization as well as to his own soul is when the leader coach can actually identify and train up his successor. Having had this opportunity several times, in all of the above referenced organizations, it is both reassuring and self-actualizing to have trained your successor, to walk away with head held high, secure in the knowledge that the organization is in good hands, and that the foundation and momentum that you have built will continue to go forward. Hopefully this does not sound egotistical, because it is not intended as such. A legacy such as this that a leader can leave his players and the organization knows no bounds in either time or possibility.

Motivation speaker Zig Ziglar is fond of saying that a person can get everything they want out of life by helping others get what they want. We believe that this too captures the essence of the character of the Leader Coach.

CONCLUSION

It would be easy to make this conversation resonate with religious overtones, and speak of the giving done on the part of Jesus Christ, Mother Theresa, Mahatma Gandhi or Martin Luther King Jr., but suffice to say that the gift of giving requires a conscious effort on the part of the Leader Coach. Because it originates on a much higher plain, it can often be the greatest reward that the coach experiences. Remember the old adage that we shared earlier that "a candle loses nothing by lighting another." Nothing can be more true of the relationship between Leader Coach and player.

Part VI

*Finale:
Assessment and Final Thoughts*

When we began writing this book, it was out of a desire to share the passion and commitment that we both feel about the art of leading and coaching people. As we wrap up these thoughts, we hope that they will have generated some excitement in your soul, and that you may close the pages of this book and feel a bit inspired about the stewardship you enjoy with those people that you call players.

To assist you in determining just where you fit into the entire Manager-Leader-Leader Coach spectrum, we have a final theory that we call the Leadership Coaching Coefficient Triangle. We hope that you will take a minute to determine your own position in the triangle, and will consider being the subject of a 360 review.

Chapter 15

Assess

The final thought that we want to leave with you is that the roles of Manager, Leader, and Leader Coach are not mutually exclusive. As we postulated in chapter 2, we believe that to achieve the status of a Leader Coach that an individual *does* have to master the inherent tasks of being a Manager and Leader. However, unlike a doctor who may elect to specialize his practice in a very narrow niche, being a Leader Coach is more like achieving a progressive rank in karate or the military, where one merely assumes more responsibility and still must maintain the skills acquired at the lesser levels. A true Leader Coach masters the skills of a Manager and a Leader, and then establishes a balance or a new inner congruence system that allows him to stay grounded in all three critical areas.

If we were to draw a diagram that depicts this theory, it would look like Figure 15.1, where the effectiveness within each role is depicted as a value on an axis with a relative measure of performance in each dimension. Obviously for the high performing, well-balanced person, the "shape" of complete development would depict a full, symmetrical triangle.

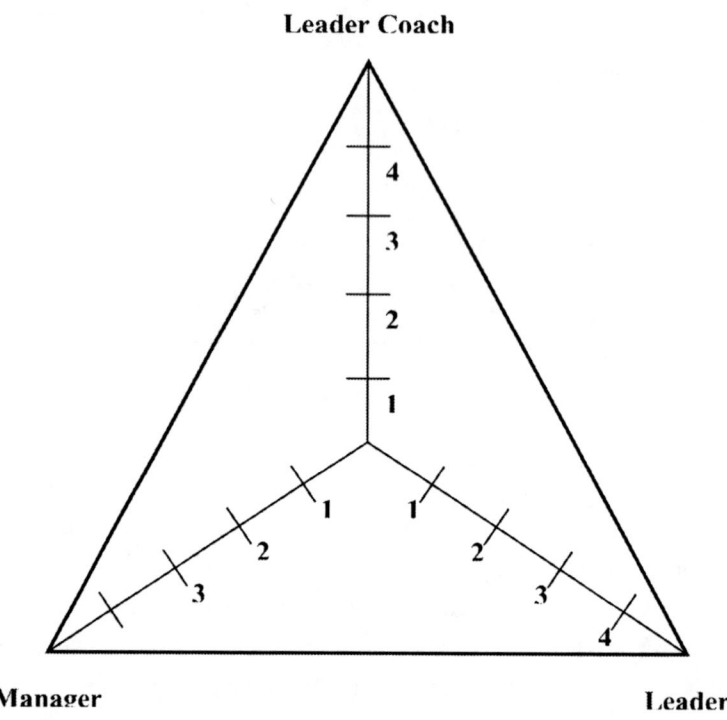

Figure 15.1 Leadership Coaching Coefficient Triangle

Of course we are all imperfect beasts, and it's a bit much to ask for us to be completely developed and perfectly symmetrical.

Relative Performance in Each Dimension

Observe that on each axis there are five levels, ranked 1 to 5, loosely denoting the following levels:

1- Low priority; almost never performs related tasks or abdicates responsibility for it (as in cases of annual reviews and other managerial forms of reporting).
2- Occasional attention; while largely ignored will perform the bare necessities.

3- Meets requirements – average performance is maintained.
4- Exceeds requirements – obviously a priority for this individual. Consistently pays attention to these tasks.
5- Always exceeds requirements; models the attributes of this portion of the triangle in every aspect of life.

With a relative rating of '5' representing the strongest tendency in an area, the *perfect* Leader Coach who had not abandoned his managerial and leadership skills and was completely balanced and developed would be rated a '15' on this scale.

WHAT COMPETENCIES DO YOU DISPLAY?

We have all worked for a charismatic leader who may have been a terrible manager, or not had a clue on how to provide us with any form of mentoring, much less coaching. Likewise, we may have worked with coaches that were absolutely wonderful, but in their zeal to coach, might fail to complete basic management tasks and reports. We've put together a quick montage of Manager, Leader, and Leader Coach scenarios, using some self-defined labels and quick development suggestions for each, as shown in Figure 15.2. We hope it will prove useful in helping you to assess your style and development needs. Do you recognize your boss? Do you recognize yourself?

Figure 15.2

Figure 15.2 Leadership Coefficient Triangle – Types and Development Needs

LCCT Shape	Name	Description	Development Needs
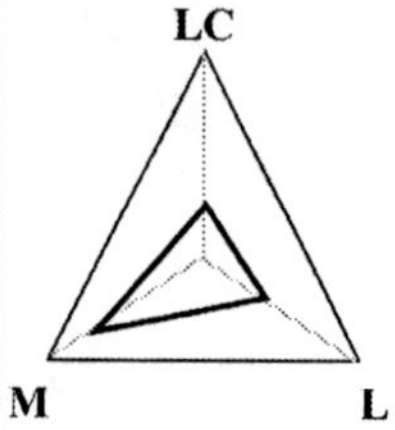 Triangle with vertices LC (top), M (bottom-left), L (bottom-right); inner triangle shown	The Administrator	Primarily measures success by completing the administrative requirements of the role. Team is not inspired by a Vision, nor receives developmental feedback other than the organization's required assessment of performance.	Focus on Vision development and vision "casting" into the managed team. Needs to develop leadership skills and presence before focusing on leader coaching.
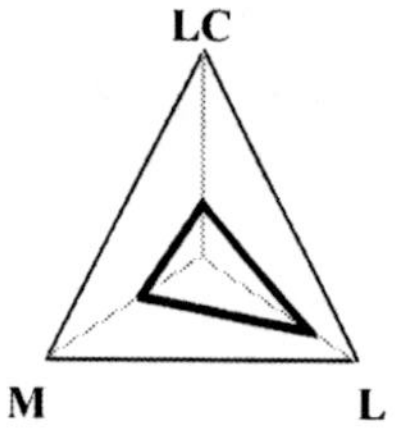 Triangle with vertices LC (top), M (bottom-left), L (bottom-right); inner triangle shown	The Dreamer	"Has his head in the clouds and his feet off the ground." Fails to execute strategies as a result of poor planning. Does not address the basic administrative requirements of the role.	Focus on the impact of not handling the fundamentals of management, such as planning and completion of assignments. May need development in basic time management and consider being more brave in giving corrective feedback to others.

LCCT Shape	Name	Description	Development Needs
	The Coach	Has great developmental conversations, but is not addressing the leadership and managerial needs of the team.	A development plan that combines the ideas for "The Dreamer" and "The Administrator" would be appropriate.
	The Beginner	Is symmetrically developed in the areas of management, leadership, and coaching; yet, has not fully developed and/or has not had the experience required for more senior roles.	Patience. Is appropriately devoting time to each role required of a leader coach, but needs more time to develop these skills.
	The Leader	Has developed a full compliment of skills, both in the areas of management and leadership and is now ready for the New Possibilities of Leader Coaching.	Read this book! Read other books on coaching as identified in the bibliography; or, attend an executive coaching class or workshop.

LCCT Shape	Name	Description	Development Needs
LC / M / L triangle	The Avoider	Similar in nature to The Dreamer. The Avoider, avoids the basic administrative requirements of the role, which may result in dropping the basic security tasks of the team or experiencing embarrassing, career limiting lapses in performance.	Work with a coach or perform some self-assessments regarding the "will" (review the Willing-Able model in Chapter 11) to do the role being asked. If appropriate consider reassignment to a role more aligned with your interest and passion.
LC / M / L triangle	The Nice Guy	Takes care of all the basics, performed on time and according to plan. Also engages his team well, focusing on their needs and growth. Does not see the need for change or is afraid of disrupting the status quo.	Similar to The Administrator, needs to focus on Vision development and Vision casting with the team. Efforts focused on coaching are noble, but that energy could be devoted to creating the future direction of the business so that the team can be inspired to want to follow and participate.

LCCT Shape	Name	Description	Development Needs
(triangle with LC at top, M at bottom-left, L at bottom-right)	The Leader Coach	Fully developed with a symmetrical skill set. Devotes time to the basic, required tasks of the role. Has created a Vision for the organization, has cast it widely, and connected team roles to its achievement. Devotes time to the coaching of the team, using the Socratic method to engage his players and expand the team's thinking.	Continue focusing on New Possibilities not only for the player's on the teams, but also focus on New Possibilities for self.

When you examine the Leadership Coaching Coefficient Triangle, remember that the leg length of anyone of the three sides can only get so small before a Leader Coach's effectiveness becomes seriously impaired. Meaning, that regardless how well one performs in one dimension, if another dimension is seriously deficient or absent, it brings into question the total competency of the Leader Coach.

How might you use this model? For now, we hope that it will serve as a tool for self-awareness and introspection. Perhaps in the future we'll develop some elaborate evaluation tool to assess your actual, current level of performance and target your development. Until then, use your self-assessment to determine what dimensions of management, leadership, and coaching you display, and create a development plan between yourself and a coach, or ideally, with *your* Leader Coach, in order to more fully develop yourself symmetrically.

Recommended Post Reading Homework

To determine if your assessment of yourself is accurate, we would heartily recommend that you arrange with your HR leader to have a 360 review assembled and completed on you. For those not familiar with the process, key personnel selected from among your subordinates, peers, and superiors are gathered to review certain key aspects of your performance. This exercise is typically moderated by an HR leader or your direct manager, and should greatly enhance the communication between you and those who participate in the exercise.

Learnings from having been the subject of a 360

- Get over the feeling of being selfish in asking for their participation.
- You, the team, and the organization are going to benefit from the process.
- Recognize that the only person that you need to be better than tomorrow is yourself.
- Encourage everyone to take it serious.
- This is a growth tool for all participating.
- Your communication will be even stronger.

The rules for participants are pretty simple:
- It is a safe room – you won't be in there – the HR leader or Manager is facilitating
- Please participate! Don't be a wallflower. Every single participant is expected to provide input. That is what makes this work. It is important that all voices are heard. Direct the HR leader or Manager to ensure that this happens.
- There should be a policy of non-attribution with the exception that you may ask the facilitator to track any extraordinary comments as coming from specific functions just so you can attach some perspective to it.

- Establish a time for you to review the results with the facilitator, so that you can respond to the feedback, and in turn, with further input from the group, formulate your go forward action plan.
- With a large group be prepared for sometimes mixed, and often time, contradictory results.
- Recognize that self improvement is a good thing, and is something that we should always be striving for as we compete with ourselves.
- Ignore the desire to want to make educated guesses as to who said what and why, because it is not relevant or germane to these proceedings.

- Do ask questions that serve as amplification or clarification; do avoid being or appearing defensive. If you are confused on some points and apparent inconsistencies, ask questions.

Some examples of how the results may be mixed and apparently contradictory would include requests or comments for you to:
- Hands off – yet controlling.
- Give us more – but be a filter.
- Give us more – but keep us in the field.
- Be a stronger decision maker – yet more empowering.
- Be more direct in writing – let us do our own thing.
- Make the tough calls – but let us take the risks.
- Don't buck the system – challenge the process.
- Love us separately – love us as a team.
- Be more organized – we plan too much.
- Don't buck the system – challenge the process.
- Give up control – be more hands on.
- Need more communication – we have too much communication.
- Individual relationships v. team.

Conclusion(s):
- If you think you were communicating well before, it will only improve exponentially.
- Don't be alarmed if there are a lot of negatives to be discussed.
- Thank participants for their candor; acknowledge it, and ask for permission to start talking as frankly and bluntly to all of those who participated.

CONCLUSION

The 360 is but one form of assessment that is available to you as a Leader Coach to gauge your effectiveness. While there are many diagnostic tools and tests that are available that will generically measure your leadership and coaching skill sets, there is nothing more effective than a 360 to compare and contrast your perceived and actual impact on your team. Don't be afraid to engage in the process, and to press the participants for nothing less than total candor. You, your team, and the organization <u>will</u> benefit from the experience.

When you examine the Leadership Coaching Coefficient Triangle, remember that any line segment can only get so small before a Leader Coach's effectiveness becomes seriously impaired. Don't think for a minute that you and or someone you are coaching is so dynamic in one dimension that it's a free pass to abandon one or two of the other dimensions.

Leadership Coaching should be the most rewarding activity in which you engage while in the work environment. If you are committed, willing to expose both your heart and soul to your players, and place the interests of others ahead of your own, it will be the best work you ever do, and may very well be your legacy.

EPILOGUE

How do you wrap up a book about being a Leader Coach? Suffice to say that we have chosen to expose our souls to you, as well as our work to your review and critique. As we said many pages ago, there are only two major forces in the universe in which we live, namely *love* (representing everything that is positive) and *fear* (representing everything that is negative). What we have discovered is that it is more about choosing our attitudes each and every morning as we awake. Are we going to have a good day or a bad one? Are we going to look at obstacles as challenges or opportunities? A story that we love, and have chosen to modify, relates the tale of three bricklayers. When asked what each is doing, the first bricklayer, whom we think of as the manager, responds, "I am laying brick." The second bricklayer, the leader, says "I am building a wall." The third bricklayer, the Leader Coach replies, "I am building a cathedral." What an amazing difference these three people displayed while going about the same task. Each of us that aspire to being a Leader Coach has the ability to be that third bricklayer. It is a matter of exercising our choices.

Back in chapter two we proposed that to achieve the top level of the pyramid of Leader Coach that an individual had to first master the tasks inherent to being a good manager, and then progress to those associated with being a leader that followers would in fact follow. In chapter 15, we took this thought to the next level and even offered you the opportunity to assess yourself. We also asked you to assess those whom you have worked for over the years, and to determine the degree to which each of these attributes have manifested themselves in those individuals. The beauty of this exercise is that we all have the choice as to which bricklayer we want to be each and every day, and how many 'points' of the Leadership Coaching Coefficient Triangle we wish to achieve in every aspect of our lives. Do we want to harness the positive energy associated with love in order to build ourselves up, as well as those around us, or will we allow the negativity associated with fear to drag us down collectively? In any event, we really do have this choice each and every day.

For this reason, we are not going to belabor the point ourselves, and rather elect to rely upon more of the wit and insights of President Theodore Roosevelt, and share what we believe is a fair summation of how the Leader Coach earns his or her spurs each and every day.

> "It is not the critic who counts; not the man who points out how the strong man stumbles, or where the doer of deeds could have done better. The credit belongs to the man who is actually in the arena, whose face is marred by dust and sweat and blood; who strives valiantly; who errs, and comes short again and again, because there is no effort without error or shortcoming; who knows the great enthusiasms, the great devotions; who spends himself in worthy cause; who at the best knows in the end the triumph of high achievement, and who at the worst, if he fails, at least fails while daring greatly, so that his place shall never be with those cold and timid souls who know neither victory nor defeat."
>
> -Theodore Roosevelt

This has been a labor of love for us, and we hope it has been of value to you.

Don

Terry

BIBLIOGRAPHY

Axelrod, Alan. *Patton on Leadership.* Paramus, NJ: Prentiss Hall Press, 2001.

Blanchard, Ken and Sheldon Bowles. *Gung Ho!* New York: William Morrow & Co, 1998.

Center for Army Leadership. *The U.S. Army Leadership Field Manual.* New York: McGraw-Hill, 2004.

Gerber, Michael E. *The E Myth Revisited.* New York: HarperCollins Publishers, Inc., 1995.

Giuliani, Rudolph W., *Leadership.* New York: Miramax Books, 2002.

Harari, Oren. *The Leadership Secrets of Colin Powell.* New York: McGraw-Hill, 2002.

Holtz, Lou. *Winning Every Day.* New York: HarperCollins, 1998.

Hunter, James C. *The Servant.* Rocklin, CA: Prima Publishing, 1998.

Jackson, Phil. *Sacred Hoops.* New York: Hyperion, 1995.

Kiyosaki, Robert T. *Rich Dad, Poor Dad*. New York: Time Warner Book Group, 1998.

Kouzes, James M and Barry Z. Posner. *Encouraging the Heart*. San Francisco, CA: Jossey-Bass, *2003*.

Kouzes, James M and Barry Z. Posner. *The Leadership Challenge*. San Francisco, CA: Jossey-Bass, *1995*.

Krisco, Kim H. *Leadership & The Art of Conversation*. Mumbai: Jaico Publishing House, 2003.

Lombardi, Vince Jr., *What It Takes To Be #1*. New York: McGraw-Hill, 2001.

Lundin, Stephen C. and Harry Paul and John Christensen. *Fish!* New York: Hyperion, 2000.

Madigan, Tim. *I'm Proud of You*. New York: Gotham Books, 2006.

Maxwell, John C. *The 21 Indispensable Qualities of a Leader*. Nashville, TN: Thomas Nelson Publishers, 1999.

Maxwell, John C. *The 21 Irrefutable Laws of Leadership*. Nashville, TN: Thomas Nelson Publishers, 1998.

Moore, Thomas. *Care of the Soul*. New York: HarperCollins Publishers, Inc., 1992.

Phillips, Donald T. *Lincoln on Leadership*. New York: Warner Books, 1992.

Pitino, Rick. *Success is a Choice*. New York: Broadway Books, 1997.

Stone, Douglas and Bruce Patton and Sheila Heen. *Difficult Conversations*. New York: Penguin Group, 1999.

Strock, James M. *Theodore Roosevelt on Leadership*. Roseville, CA: Prima Publishing, 2001.

Torre, Joe. *Joe Torre's Ground Rules for Winners*. New York: Hyperion, 1999.

Waitley, Denis. *Seeds of Greatness*. New York: Simon & Schuster, Inc., 1983.

Warren, Rick. *The Purpose Driven Life*. Grand Rapids, MI: Zondervan, 2002.

Whitworth, Laura and Henry Kimsey-House and Phil Sandahl. *Co-Active Coaching*. Palo Alto, CA: Davies-Black Publishing, 1998.

About The Authors

Don Levin, is a former Attorney at Law with over thirteen years of general practice experience, and nine years as a court appointed arbitrator. He is also a retired U.S. Army officer, with over twenty three years of commissioned service spent in a variety of command and staff positions, twelve years of which were at the General Staff level. He is also a past senior sales leader for two Fortune 200 companies.

Don earned his JD from The John Marshall Law School, his MPA from the University of Oklahoma, and a BA from the University of Illinois-Chicago. He is also a graduate of the U.S. Army Command & General Staff College and the Defense Strategy Course, U.S. Army War College.

Don is very active with his church and within the community, and resides with his wife Susie, in Richmond, VA. They have five children and seven grandchildren. In his spare time, Don enjoys other forms of writing, and is about to release a third fiction novel, and is working on a lessons in leadership book.

Terry Edwards is a senior executive with twenty-six years of diverse leadership experience ranging from seventeen years with three Fortune 200 sized companies, and sailing as a tugboat captain and as a regimental officer at the United States Merchant Marine Academy at Kings Point, NY. In addition to the requisite skills of any large organizational leader, he specializes in change leadership and leadership coaching and development.

Terry received his MBA from Boston University and BS from Kings Point. He completed the Leadership Coaching graduate certificate program at Georgetown University where he is an adjunct faculty member.

Terry is currently a Boy Scout leader, and he and his wife Susan reside in Richmond, VA where they are raising their three sons. Terry still enjoys getting out on the water and editing books at Starbucks with Don.

You may reach Don and Terry, or speak to us about our various workshops and programs for your next corporate, vendor, or leadership meeting by visiting the Legacy Search LLC website at: www.legacysrch.com.

Watch for *The Family Coach: Exposing Your Heart* **in the near future.**

Printed in the United States
71469LV00003BA/134